Revealed Masters 19th Century American Art

William H. Gerdts

*Professor of Art, Brooklyn College
of The City University of New York*

An Exhibition organized by
The American Federation of Arts, New York

This exhibition and publication are
supported by a special grant from
the National Endowment for the Arts.

Published by The American Federation of Arts
41 East 65th Street, New York, N. Y.

Library of Congress Catalog Number 74-16549
AFA Exhibition Number 74-1
Circulated September, 1974-September, 1975

Catalogue designed by Michael Shroyer

Produced in Los Angeles
by Tom Kellaway,
American Art Review Press.

Contents

Photograph Credits

Armen Photographers, Newark: 2, 34, 41
Armstrong Browning Library, Waco: 22
N. E. Baldwin, Schenectady: 25
The Brooklyn Museum: 23
Cincinnati Art Museum: 16
Geoffrey Clements, New York: 3, 19, 40
The Detroit Institute of Arts: 32
Flint Institute of Arts: 38
Greenberg & May, Buffalo: 36
Helga Photo Studio, Inc., New York: 35
Indianapolis Museum of Art: 15
The J. B. Speed Art Museum, Louisville: 10
Stuart Lynn, New Orleans: 7
The Metropolitan Museum of Art, New York: 28, 30
Museum of Fine Arts, Boston: cover, 1, 11, 12, 20, 39
National Collection of Fine Arts, Washington: 37
O. E. Nelson, New York: 8, 13, 14, 24, 27, 29, 33, 42, 43
Newark Museum: 9
Pennsylvania Academy of the Fine Arts: 21
Philadelphia Museum of Art, A. J. Wyatt: 17
Unknown: 4, 5
Jean Winnie, Cooperstown: 6
Yale University Art Gallery, Joseph Szaszfai: 18, 26, 31

The Color Plates were produced from
photographs taken by Geoffrey Clements

Acknowledgements

In the last two decades, a renewed interest and appreciation has brought considerable popular attention to such 19th-century American masters as Homer and Eakins. However, the history of American painting of that period is filled with names which today are unfamiliar even to many scholars in the field. Many artists who were regularly shown in the important exhibitions of the time are now relatively unknown and are being re-discovered and re-evaluated. Some of these artists created only one, two or at most a very few works of importance; others, an extensive body of work. This publication and exhibition survey 19th-century American art through the portraiture, landscape, still-life, genre and grand-manner painting of these little-known artists.

The American Federation of Arts is particularly indebted to Dr. William H. Gerdts, Professor of Art at Brooklyn College of The City University of New York, who conceived of the theme for this project, selected the works to be included and wrote this catalogue. Professor Theodore H. Stebbins, Curator of American Painting and Sculpture, Yale University, assisted him in this selection, and Doreen Bolger, student and Fellow of the City University Graduate Center, prepared the biographies and bibliographies for each of the artists. Jane Fluegel of the Museum of Modern Art ably edited the catalogue. Without their combined efforts this project could not have been realized.

Our special thanks are due to Thomas R. Kellaway of the *American Art Review* for generously contributing the color plates.

I am also grateful to the following American Federation of Arts' staff: to Konrad G. Kuchel, who coordinated all aspects of the exhibition; to Jane Tai, for scheduling the tour and assistance in editing the catalogue; to Melissa Meighan, AFA Registrar, who also assisted in editing the publication; to Susie D'Alton for typing the manuscript; to Lynn Allegaert, for arranging the publicity and members' events for the tour; to Mary Ann Monet, for producing the special typography for the publication; and, finally, to Michael Shroyer, for designing the catalogue and exhibition graphics.

The exhibition and catalogue are supported by a generous grant from the National Endowment for the Arts.

Wilder Green
Director

Revealed Masters

The dominant tradition in American painting during the 17th and 18th centuries was portraiture. It is probably true that other themes were more widely explored than is usually recognized today, and certainly paintings and engravings that were not portraits were imported from Europe by Colonial settlers, but nevertheless, the portrait — sometimes of family and loved ones, sometimes of significant leaders of political, military and religious life — remained the primary staple for pictorial activity.

19th-century portraiture and its mid-century changes

The situation did not immediately change in the early 19th century. Indeed, the exhibition records of the newly founded organizations such as New York's American Academy of the Fine Arts and the later National Academy of Design, and Philadelphia's Pennsylvania Academy of the Fine Arts, show a preponderance of portraits, and, in fact, the support of the art-union lottery organizations and their annual exhibitions in the 1840s came about in part as a revolt against the entrenched officialdom of the older institutions and their proclivity to portraiture. As the complaint was often stated in the press at the time: "Portraits, portraits, nothing but portraits!"

After about 1840, however, the primacy of portraiture declined, and declined rather rapidly. This, and its attendant decline in quality and originality, has often been attributed to the development and the popularity of the camera, but this would seem to oversimplify greatly the problem of this phenomenon. For one thing, the photograph might only have increased the popularity of portraiture, and the painted portrait was still vastly superior to the photographic counterpart, both in terms of color and the ability of the portrait painter to create a work in life size. Rather, this change in attitude toward the portrait art, while allied with photography, seems instead to herald a more scientific attitude toward the depiction of the individual. The emphasis upon individual characterization in mid-century portraiture, as opposed to the embodiment of certain ideal qualities of beauty, nobility of soul, and intellectual superiority, which characterize late 18th- and early 19th-century portraiture on both sides of the Atlantic, may signify the decline of a basically neoclassic belief in unchanging values, and the substitution of a Darwinian scientific spirit, recognizing change and flux as basic to the human condition. As the dominance of man's position within a world of manifold forms and elements declined, so the art form devoted solely to his appearance lost its superior place, giving way to an emphasis on the one hand to the situations, sometimes humorous and satirical, characteristic of his transient condition in this changing world, and on the other to the appearance of that world itself — that is, the landscape, and in turn *its* product — the still life.

Beginning of genre, landscape, and still life

In a sense, then, the early 19th-century portrait painters who flourished within the aesthetic of idealizing portraiture, men such as Thomas Sully in Philadelphia and Henry Inman in New York, may be seen as the end of a noble tradition that goes back through Gilbert Stuart and Sir Thomas Lawrence to Sir Joshua Reynolds, Thomas Gainsborough and ultimately to Sir Anthony Van Dyck. But while Sully and Inman — each of whom was sometimes called the "American Lawrence" — were the most famous and most respected American portraitists of the early 19th century, there were numerous others of high professional ability whose achievements at times equaled those of their more famous contemporaries. Manuel Joachim de Franca was one of these, his Portuguese background (he was born either in Oporto on the mainland or on the island of Madeira) adding an exotic element to his practice of portrait painting in Philadelphia. It is not known whether de Franca was familiar with the art of his earlier countryman, Francisco Vieira, who worked in Oporto and died in Funchal, or with painting of the most famous Portuguese painter of the period, Domingos Antonio de Sequeira, but both artists painted portraits as well as religious works. Therein may lie the origins of de Franca's art, for he appears in Philadelphia in 1830, already a trained and practicing painter of portraits, and also of religious pictures, before moving on to St. Louis in the 1840s. De Franca at first met difficulties in obtaining sitters in Philadelphia, owing to his unfamiliarity with the English language, but he soon became a part of the local art establishment, and upon forming a close friendship with the English-born and trained landscape painter, Joshua Shaw, not only collaborated with him but helped to organize with him in 1837 the Artists' and Amateurs' Association. De Franca's *Portrait of Matthew Hinzinga Messchert,* 1839 (cat. no. 17), maintains the romantic charm of innocent childhood that one identifies with the portraiture of his better-known Philadelphia contemporaries, Sully and John Neagle; the latter also painted members of the Messchert family.

Early still life

Another Philadelphia portraitist was Robert Street, who began exhibiting there as early as 1815. Street's portraits are usually severe and stiff, falling into that ambiguous category of "semi-professional" or "semi-primitive." Street, however, occasionally painted other subjects, investigating religious, landscape, and still-life themes. *The Basket of Apples,* 1818 (cat. no. 38), is just about the only still life by him known today, though he exhibited one at the Pennsylvania Academy in 1859. Street's apple picture is like his portraits — linear, simplified and stark.

This little picture is an early testimonial to the rise of still-life painting as an independent American genre — independent, that is, of the portrait to which it formerly had been merely an accessory. Still-life painting remained at the bottom of the qualitative ladder in the constructions of the academic theoreticians of the 17th and 18th centuries. History, or grand-manner, painting was considered the most meaningful, for it called upon the imaginative powers of the artist and at the same time could provide moral instruction. Portraiture came next, but still life was least significant, deemed only a mere transcription of nature.

Origins of American still life

Thus when still-life painting began in America, it was a humble theme of scant remuneration. Its origins are closely tied to Street's native city, Philadelphia, for it was in the hands of the various artist-members of the Peale family that still-life painting began. Probably the finest specialist in this theme was Raphaelle Peale, the eldest son of Charles Willson Peale. Raphaelle Peale's still lifes bear many similarities to this near-unique work by Street. Both artists emphasize an abstract geometry of form, favoring perfect spheres and ovals, here seen in both the fruit and the wire basket containing the apples. Both emphasize symmetry and formal composition; both concentrate upon linear sharpness. While Street's still life does not have the sophistication of the finest of those by Raphaelle Peale, it would satisfy the aesthetics of neoclassicism, were it not for the neoclassic disdain for the still life as being devoid of moral or ideal significance.

Still-life painting had a tentative beginning in the early years of the 19th century in America, but it began to flower in the middle of the century. This is due in part to the country's increased affluence, which is directly reflected in the richness of the still-life subjects. It was due also to the establishment of the art-unions and their encouragement of themes that could be universally understood and appreciated; in view of the art-unions' distribution of works of art by lottery, they could not usually choose portraits. Finally, it was due to the stimulation given to many areas of art by the influx of European painters in the wake of the liberal revolutions in Europe in 1848.

One of the most able and most successful mid-century still-life specialists was William Mason Brown. His artistic career reflects the changes and development in American painting of the 19th century. His early works of the 1850s are landscapes, rather free and painterly in manner, reflecting the art of Thomas Cole or the early Jasper Cropsey. But sometime in the mid-1860s he turned to still life, seemingly rather abruptly, and his style changed to a very precise, almost photographic mode, in keeping with the mid-century aesthetic. Brown's success as a painter for chromolithographic reproduction may also account for his change of style for it was the sale of his *Basket of Peaches, Upset* to the New York art dealer William Schaus, at a price of $2,000 for the purpose of reproduction, that first brought Brown fame.

Still lifes in a natural setting

Some of Brown's pictures are table-top still lifes, often filled with bric-a-brac, but he was also one of the major exponents of a "new" form of still life, the return-to-nature picture. Herein, occasionally flowers but usually fruit were placed in a natural setting, in a glade of nature, often sitting directly upon the ground or on a cushion of leaves, but sometimes tumbling from rustic containers such as wicker baskets or straw hats. Such was the setting of the Schaus picture mentioned above, but Brown, and his contemporaries who indulged in this form of still life, usually favored smaller objects — berries, cherries and the like, as in *Raspberries* (cat. no. 10). This still-life form began in America in the 1860s and reflects the significance of the writing of John Ruskin to American as well as English artists, for it was Ruskin who pronounced against the artificiality of the Dutch table-top still-life tradition and favored the supposedly more natural presentation of "flowers relieved by grass or moss, and fruit-tree blossoms relieved against the sky." The still life, then, should seem to be come upon accidentally, and growing objects should be set in their original, more "natural" and "truthful" setting.

Influence of John Ruskin

Thus, the popular fruit subject matter was shown lying on the ground in the woods. The floral equivalent, as suggested by Ruskin, would be to depict growing flowers in a garden with sunlight and air. This was one form of flower painting practiced by George Lambdin at the mid-century. Lambdin was a Philadelphia painter who had first painted genre subjects but gradually, in the 1860s, moved more and more toward still life. He never abandoned his earlier interest in genre, and sometimes successfully combined the two. He was one of the most noted still-life artists of the mid-century and the best known painter of flowers. Floral still lifes were not common in the early years of the century in this country, but after the 1850s, the number of flower paintings appearing in exhibitions was constantly on the increase, eventually exceeding the fruit pictures. Although Lambdin painted a large number of traditional bouquets in vases — table-top pictures — he seems particularly responsible for the development in America of the outdoor flower picture. An example of the latter is *Roses,* 1874 (cat. no. 24). His works tend toward a softer and slightly sweeter treatment than the tight, precise forms of Brown. His models for these outdoor garden pictures were easily enough found, for he had a particularly well-known and admired rose garden of his own at his Philadelphia home; it is not surprising that the rose is the flower he most favored.

*Hunting and
fishing still lifes*

One other category of still life with significant practitioners was that depicting the trophies of the hunt and the stream. Here a once highly honored specialist was Samuel Marsden Brookes, also one of the finest painters working in California from the 1860s on. Brookes had lived in Wisconsin and began painting portraits there, but he turned to still lifes, particularly fish pictures, once he settled in San Francisco in 1862. *Still Life* (cat. no. 8) of that year is thus one of the first in this line and one of the first pictures he painted in California. It is also one of the most grandly orchestrated and reveals an intelligent understanding of the still-life tradition of such 17th-century Low Country specialists as Frans Snyders and Jan Fyt. It appears to be the earliest work by a California artist to have been acquired by the patron Judge E.B. Crocker, who subsequently purchased paintings by most of the leading California resident artists of note in the 1860s and 1870s.

*Rise of landscape
painting and the
Hudson River school*

The most important thematic development of the 1820s, however, of far greater impact and critical acclaim than still-life painting, was the rise of a native school of landscape painting. Called, even then, and still, I believe, something of a misnomer, the "Hudson River school," it lasted for many decades and encompassed several generations of able painters of actually widely diverse aesthetic reactions to nature; some of these, such as Thomas Cole, Asher B. Durand, Frederic Church, and the several Luminist painters, are well known today. One such painter was David Johnson, a pupil of a "second-generation" Hudson-River-school artist, Jasper Cropsey. Johnson is typical of the better-than-average landscapist who could, at times, produce minor masterworks. The majority of the paintings that have come to the fore in recent years — and there has been a minor Johnson revival recently — have been his later works, those from 1870 on. These are attractive enough pictures, but they are generally without special distinction and mark Johnson as something of a modified Barbizon-type American artist, with a close-keyed tonality somewhat sparkling brushwork and a concern for air and atmosphere rather than topographical exactitude or distinction. But some of his early pictures, done at the time of his study with the far-better-known Cropsey or shortly thereafter, and thus much more in the earlier style of mid-century realism and scientific exactitude, are real gems. One of the finest of these is the *Old Mill, West Milford, New Jersey,* 1850 (cat. no. 23), and very likely this was done under Cropsey's tutelage, since West Milford is very near Greenwood Lake, where Cropsey had found a favorite painting subject, a summer home, and a wife. Here, a concern with picturesque subject is allied to specificity of region and of individual objects, yet without the loss of monumental form or sacrifice of vivid brushwork. Johnson's dramatic use of light and control of color are greater than his teacher's and, in a curious way, parallel some of the qualities of French Realism.

David Johnson was based in New York City and much of his landscape painting was done in the New York area. Alexander Lawrie was also a New York landscape painter, though he had earlier lived in Philadelphia and studied abroad in Düsseldorf, Paris, and Florence. In Philadelphia he had painted primarily portraits, and he seems to have reverted to that theme in the 1870s; his best-known picture, however, is a mid-1860s interior genre piece. But on his return from a second trip abroad, after the Civil War, he seems to have felt a need to renew his association with his native land and painted a series of Adirondack landscapes in Essex County and on the Boquet River in northern New York State. The present work, *Pleasant Valley, Essex County, New York,* 1867 (cat. no. 26), is one of these.

A good deal older than either Johnson or Lawrie was Samuel Lancaster Gerry, whose landscape *Sunset* (cat. no. 19) is shown here. Though he, too, is often called a Hudson-River-school artist, his entire career, with the exception of several trips abroad, is associated with New England. His studio was in Boston, but the region he painted most was rural New England, particularly the White Mountains. He was one of a whole group of artists, both resident and visiting landscape painters, who created a kind of "White Mountain school," though the name should imply a homogeneity of topographical subject rather than any style distinct from that of the painters in the Hudson River Valley and cohesive unto itself. Gerry's works are generally placid and gently romantic; he preferred the peaceful and the harmonious to the dramatic tumult of, say Thomas Cole, and yet at times his art could rise to such a professional level as to be confused with that of Asher B. Durand.

White Mountain school

The mid-century painter was cautioned by the increasingly nationalistic art critics, as well as by some of his patrons, to remain steadfast in his Americanism and to shun Europe — its philosophy and ideals, its examples and influences, its subject matter and even the lure of traveling there. Gerry, like Durand and most of his contemporaries, honored this injunction more by the breach, in certain respects, but in the main he sought out native subject matter and painted it in quiet optimism. A number of other mid-century landscape painters, however, chose to ignore this strong and stern advice and settled in Italy for most of their mature careers. Two of these are George Loring Brown and a younger artist, John Rollin Tilton. Such artists could be sure of American patronage, not only through annual exhibitions in the larger American cities to which they might send home occasional pictures, but also from American travelers making their grand tours abroad, for whom visits to the studios of artists — primarily *American* sculptors and painters — were just about obligatory. These American travelers usually purchased one or more souvenirs of their visits — partly to lend encouragement to their fellow nationals who were laboring in an international art world among painters and sculptors of all nations; partly as proof on their return home of their concern with culture and the arts; and, of course, partly as a pictorial record of the natural beauties, the man-made wonders, and the ruins they had romantically contemplated, thus assuring the landscape specialists particular support.

Mid-century expatriate artists

Nevertheless, it is precisely this group of landscape painters who, though they may have been patronized by admiring Americans and men-

11

tioned in American periodicals in "Notes from Abroad," fell most quickly into obscurity and even oblivion, not having an American residence from which constantly to prod the art critics and historians, and probably, too, because their expatriation was an implied rejection of the myth of the superiority of the American Eden. Perhaps, also, because they were not in constant contact with the growing realism of the mid-century, these landscape painters maintained a romantic interpretation of nature longer than their counterparts at home. They painted with an emotional reaction to nature's "moods," in a technique more dramatic and painterly, in forms more generalized, than found in America.

Brown went to Europe in 1832, studying in Paris — one of the first American artists to do so — and spent much of his time at the Louvre, where he became an ardent admirer of the landscape painting of Claude Lorrain, whose works he copied on commission from the Boston Athenaeum. Brown returned home in 1834, but by 1840, with the encouragement of Washington Allston, who admired Brown's copies of Claude, he returned to Europe, this time spending almost twenty years in Italy, principally Florence and Rome. The American's admiration for Claude, who had painted so many Italian landscapes, led not only to the nickname "Claude" Brown, but also to his naming one of his sons Claude. Although the two artists shared a love of the Italian landscape, the American's paintings are far more romantic than the French 17th-century artist's. *Tivoli,* 1850 (cat. no. 9), is one of Brown's most complete "souvenirs" of Italy. Tivoli, outside of Rome, was a favorite tourist spot for Americans and others. The town and its antique ruins are clearly visible, but the total landscape is here also — the high mountains, the plunging waterfall, the deep valley, the local flora, and a picturesque Italian peasant with his dog. The work is Claudian in its repoussoir elements and centralized composition, but it is far more dramatic, more romantic and painterly.

Brown painted from Naples to Venice, and was one of the earliest Americans to explore the latter city. On his return to the Boston area in 1859, he attempted to adapt his art to a more national sentiment in style and subject, but his heart remained in Arcadian Italy. The pastiches he painted of Italian subjects back in his Malden studio are pale and lifeless reflections of his once vital art. Nathaniel Hawthorne wrote in his Italian notebooks an amusing description of Brown, which, in its emphasis upon Brown's "Yankeeness," may explain why the artist did not suffer total neglect as did his fellow expatriate, Tilton:

> We have been recently to the studio of Mr. Brown the American
> landscape painter, and were altogether surprised and delighted
> with his pictures. He is a plain, homely Yankee, quite unpolish-
> ed by his many years' residence in Italy; he talks ungrammati-
> cally, and in Yankee idioms; walks with a strange, awkward gait
> and stooping shoulders; is altogether unpicturesque; but wins
> one's confidence by his very lack of grace. It is not often that
> we see an artist so entirely free from affectation in his aspect
> and deportment. His pictures were views of Swiss and Italian
> scenery, and were most beautiful and true. ...I suppose Claude
> was a greater landscape painter than Brown; but for my own
> pleasure I would prefer one of the latter artist's pictures.

Brown's work and his life are known today. John Rollin Tilton is a forgotten figure in the history of art. This is all the more surprising since his name arises rather frequently in the contemporary American periodicals, reports of the activities of expatriates, but scarcely any of his landscapes has so far emerged. Perhaps this is because he never returned to America. He lived in Italy from 1852 until his death, traveling through Europe and to Egypt, and becoming even more than Brown an integral part of the expatriate colony. A close friend of the successful American sculptor in Rome, William Wetmore Story, he painted *Landscape (Italian Ruins),* (cat. no. 40), for his colleague. Both artists, in fact, had rooms in the Palazzo Barberini in Rome. The sense of noble desolation in this painting, the dramatic positioning of its commanding tower, seen from a "frog's-eye view," is astonishing, but it is impossible to judge whether this is typical of Tilton's superior artistry or is an exceptional example of his talents.

The painting *Buffalo Harbor from the Foot of Porter Avenue,* 1871 (cat. no. 36), by Lars Sellstedt is the major work of that too-little-known artist. Sellstedt is a primary exemplar of the idea that regional aspects of American art are deserving of further investigation. Sellstedt's biography reads like a 19th-century romance: he was born to a prosperous and educated family in Sundsvall, Sweden, but his resentment of his stepfather led him to run away to sea. After thirteen years at sea, he decided upon the more profitable alternative of being a lake sailor, which in turn led him to Buffalo. There he amused himself as a painter and sailed Lake Erie. A meeting with Thomas Le Clear led him to the profession of artist. Sellstedt was a leader in artistic circles in Buffalo, active in organizing the Buffalo Fine Arts Academy, and a close friend of all the local painters; for a while he shared a studio with William H. Beard, whose work is also included here. His activities are perceptively and delightfully documented in his various writings.

Art in Buffalo

Sellstedt seems to have been active principally as a portrait painter, certainly the art form most in demand in Buffalo, but *Buffalo Harbor* is his best known work. Here he is able to combine the meticulous attention to detail with a sense of the flat, limitless space of the Lake harbor. He has produced a really panoramic monument to his adopted city and to the marine activity which was the early basis of his career.

Buffalo artists were still related to and often exhibited with the Eastern art establishment, despite the difficulties of time and distance in the 19th century. Probably the two most independent and therefore most interesting regional schools were in New Orleans and in California, the latter centered principally in San Francisco, developing after the Gold Rush. The activities there of the still-life painter Samuel Marsden Brookes have already been noted. A landscape painter of note was Fortunato Arriola. Like Sellstedt, Arriola was an immigrant to America, in this case from Mexico. He arrived in San Francisco in 1857 and remained there until 1871, when he went to New York in search of further recognition. He died a year later by drowning when the ship on which he was returning to California caught fire in the Atlantic.

California school

Arriola was a portraitist but principally a landscape painter. *California Landscape* (cat. no. 3) is one of his relatively rare California scenes. Moreover, and even rarer it would seem in California art, it is

13

luminist in style. The clarity of forms together with the all-pervading luminescence, the sense of a stopped moment in time, even the forms of the boats themselves, markers in the reflecting pool of water, can be paralleled in the work of the well-known Eastern Luminists, Martin Johnson Heade and Fitz Hugh Lane. Even the foreground grasses and the sharp linear outlines along the edge of the water are similar to the nubbly rocks marking the foregrounds of Heade's beach scenes.

Romanticism and the tropics

Most of Arriola's landscapes, however, are not of the rugged landscape of California or the spectacular mountains of the West painted by Albert Bierstadt, Thomas Hill, and others, but tropical reminiscences done from memory. These were not necessarily even of Mexico; a number are Central American. The experience of traveling through the tropical jungles across the Isthmus of Panama was familiar to many of the settlers in California, and while that experience was seldom a pleasant one, and thus not likely to inspire romantic pictorial nostalgia, the success of Frederic Church's South American paintings led to a new appreciation of that landscape. The description of that landscape by the German naturalist, Alexander von Humboldt, had inspired Church's trips to South America. It is significant that in 1869, the centennial of Humboldt's birth, there was a great fair in San Francisco where tropical landscapes were much in evidence. In fact, landscapes by California artists of Latin American subjects in turn became popular in the East, and the two works Arriola exhibited in New York the year of his death were Mexican views.

To some who saw America as a new Garden of Eden at mid-century, South America seemed even more untainted, more "natural" as God made it, than the already heavily settled North American continent. This vision accounts in part for the phenomenal success of Frederic Church, who surely is the greatest 19th-century interpreter of the sister continent.

Accompanying Church on his second trip to Ecuador in 1857, was Louis Remy Mignot, a Charleston-born artist who worked in New York until moving to England at the beginning of the Civil War. Mignot's *On the Guayaquil* (cat. no. 29) stems from that journey. Mignot did not have the vision of grandeur that was uniquely Church's, and his South American scenes may be thought derivative, but they have a rich vitality and exciting colorism that mark the artist at his best as a first rate, if neglected, master.

Jervis McEntee was a pupil of Church's. Although McEntee is usually considered a painter of the second generation of Hudson-River-school landscapists, his art quite strongly veers away from the topographical precision and detail of the orthodox artists of that movement. He never aspired to the cosmic vision of his teacher, and while through the influence of Church he may have maintained a certain concern with the specific, he moved more and more into paintings of mood — gently melancholic landscapes with an emphasis on sparse, November twilight scenes (later to become the specialty of a number of end-of-the-century painters such as John Enneking and Hugh Bolton Jones). In *A Skating Party,* 1890 (cat. no. 27), McEntee is painting a landscape-cum-genre, which was itself a popular subject in late-19th-century American art, featured in works by other, lesser-known painters such as Johann Culverhouse and John O'Brien Inman.

Romantic tendencies, as opposed to the dominant mid-19th-century

14

realism, are perhaps most marked in the marine painting of James Hamilton. In view of the admiration of his day for the meticulous, careful surfaces and detail-by-detail art of Church and Bierstadt, Hamilton's contemporanious excursion into full-bodied romanticism is astonishing. Still, Hamilton was born near Belfast, and his background in the British Isles may account for his aesthetic predilections; the roots of his style — the swirling, painterly compositions, the dissolution of solid matter into the engulfing forces of water, wind, clouds, and fire — are Turneresque, while the theme of civilization's destruction, to be seen in his most famous canvas, *The Last Days of Pompeii,* 1864, bears similarities to the works of John Martin and Francis Danby which cannot be mere coincidence.

Marine painting in the romantic tradition

But Hamilton was not a British artist; he was the leading marine painter in Philadelphia, where the family settled in 1834 when the young man was fifteen. Hamilton's greatest pictorial dramas are intimately associated with the Civil War, and were spectacular embodiments of that fearsome holocaust. Some are real battle scenes, such as those portraying the action between the "Monitor" and the "Merrimac." But far more significant are his symbolic works. For, is not the *Pompeii* — a picture of the destruction of a wealthy and secure civilization, parallel to the destruction engulfing the United States — a picture of the dissolution of the American dream of a new Eden? And is not *Old Ironsides* of the previous year, as well as its near-replica, *Foundering,* also of 1863, a picture of the ship of state, storm-tossed, on the brink of destruction, amidst a calamitous and cosmic storm? This message was not only reinforced by the poem by Oliver Wendell Holmes inscribed on the reverse of the painting, but, more immediately, by the second showing of the picture in 1864, when it was entitled *Shipwreck of Old Ironsides.* This exhibition was held at the Great Central Fair for the United States Sanitary Commission in Philadelphia — a benefit specifically for the equivalent of Red Cross relief during the civil struggle.

The major thematic development in American painting at the mid-century was the rise and popularity of genre painting — that is, scenes of everyday life. If Washington Allston, the painter of high ideals, was the most respected American artist in the 1830s, some ten or fifteen years later that position was assumed by William Sidney Mount, an artist of native and natural American scenes. Furthermore, the same magazines which in the 1830s condemned Mount's art for being too vulgar in its expression of raw truths would praise him at great length ten years later for exactly this same quality — albeit somewhat differently expressed — his truth to nature, his honesty, and the like.

Genre painting

The reasons for this change, even reversal in aesthetic judgments and standards are extremely complex, and much analysis still remains to be done. One can, as with other themes, point to the rise of the art-unions and their aid in propagating art "for the masses" (though this means, of course, middle-class "masses"). More significant, however, was the new nationalistic spirit of the age, the search for a message and meaning that were distinctively "American." That is not to say that the earliest American genre painters were totally uninfluenced by European prototypes. John Lewis Krimmel has been called the "American Hogarth," and the parallels between the works of Mount and Sir David Wilkie were obvious even in Mount's own times; moreover, Wilkie's influence has been traced in the paintings of Krimmel and George Caleb Bingham.

The problem involved the "telling of stories" that would speak a particularly and peculiarly American tale. Genre painting had been preceded in America by the development of genre fiction. Sir Walter Scott had proved that the novel of manners and sentiment could be adapted to portray qualities peculiar to a nation and a people — and his novels were extremely popular in America. James Fenimore Cooper proved that fiction could encompass situations and experiences unique to America, howevermuch he might owe to Scott; and in turn Cooper's involvement with American artistic development is no coincidence. Nor is the involvement of American artists with the illustration of Cooper's, and Washington Irving's, fiction. Although such painting is not, strictly speaking, genre painting, both forms have close similarities when they involve narrative.

America was peculiar, distinct, and especially, better. Her people were diverse, but class distinction was much less oppressive than in Europe; her people were happy, sometimes mischievous, but never really evil; they were content and harmonious with the land upon which they had settled. True, certain aspects of European "corruption" may have tainted our cities, but the country — not only the wilderness but especially the rural areas — embodied the finest qualities and virtues of this new American Eden. It was upon such fictions and myths that American genre developed.

Since the great majority of our early genre paintings concerned rural America, shown to be healthy and good-natured, it is not surprising that such a description would apply to the art of Mount and Bingham, our best-known genre specialists of the age. But there were many other genre painters, each with his own distinct qualities, and some who are today inexplicably neglected. One such early specialist was George H. Comegys, a Philadelphia painter about whom little is known, including his dates of birth and death. He was active, however, from the late 1830s to the early 1850s. Judging from early descriptions as well as from works that are extant, most of Comegys's pictures appear to involve children. *Boys Stealing Watermelons* (cat. no. 13) is one of these works. This choice of subject matter is characteristic of much American genre. This, too, is not surprising, for childhood involves "youth" and "newness," features of America in general and of our cultural expression in particular: our forests are "fresh and verdant," our nation is "new and unfettered by tradition." (The fact that so many American paintings are concerned with newness is a feature worthy of investigation in itself.) Comegys seems to be our earliest genre painter to have specialized in the "comic" genre, a form usually associated with the slightly later, better-known, Pittsburgh artist, David Blythe. Like Blythe, Comegys depicts situations particularly humorous in themselves with exaggerations of form, pose, gesture, and expression that verges on caricature; all is expressed in a dramatic chiaroscuro and a rich, colorful, painterly technique, which mark him as an artist of the romantic generation.

A romantic subject peculiar to our land is the painting of America's aboriginal inhabitants, the Indians; and their depiction in Louisiana is even more exotic. Some of the Indian paintings of George Catlin, Seth Eastman, and others are "genre" in that they are scenes of everyday life

3. Fortunato Arriola, *California Landscape*

4. James Henry Beard, *The Parson's Pets*

10. William Mason Brown, *Raspberries*

6. Robert Blum, *The Italian Bead Stringers*

34. Thomas P. Rossiter, *Such is Life, A Scene in London During the Crimean War*

8. Samuel Marsden Brookes, *Still Life*

35. Christian Schussele, *The Young Recruits (Mock Army)*

41. Allen Tucker, *Cornshucks and Windmill*

of a distinct segment of the population. Others, of course, are not, for they relate to specific events or to rare adventures. The grandest of all paintings of the Southern Indians is *Louisiana Indians Walking Along the Bayou,* 1847 (cat. no. 7), by the little-known Alfred Boisseau, a Parisian artist. He had exhibited in Paris before arriving in New Orleans by 1845 and he may have shown *Louisiana Indians* in the Paris Salon of 1847. A teacher as well as a painter of portraits and landscapes, Boisseau was a peripatetic man; he worked in New York and Cleveland, and died in Montreal, but he is best remembered for his activity in New Orleans, to which, indeed, a great many French artists migrated in the 19th century. Boisseau's study with the French academician, Paul Delaroche, is reflected in the strong figure construction here, and his latter-day neoclassic training is responsible for the frieze-like arrangement of the composition; yet he has at the same time successfully captured the essence of the Louisiana bayou country.

As genre developed in American painting, it sometimes affected the presentation of other themes also. Its elements played an ever-increasing role in the landscapes of some mid-century painters, and there also appeared genre-portraits — that is, paintings representing seemingly everyday scenes but in which the subjects, however spontaneously they are caught rather than formally posed, are nevertheless specific persons. Such is true of Robert W. Weir's *The Microscope* of 1849 (cat. no. 43). Weir is best known for his painting the *Embarkation of the Pilgrims* in the Rotunda of the United States Capitol. His reputation was based primarily upon his role as an artist of history subjects, but he was equally at home in portraiture, landscape, and genre. He was also a major teacher in the history of American art, a professor of drawing at West Point from 1834 to 1876, as well as the father of John and Julian Alden Weir, the latter an American Impressionist destined to exceed his father in fame. *Influence of genre painting on landscape and portraiture*

The Microscope is a relaxed, informal portrait of Jacob W. Bailey, Professor of Chemistry at West Point, and his family, appropriately centering on a moment in scientific research. A friend and colleague of Weir's, Bailey achieved fame in his microscopic research of crystals and algae. This genre-portrait is also a kind of allegorical picture, for the costumes of the figures are not contemporary but generalized interpretations of Renaissance dress. In all likelihood the painting refers to the role of the famous scientist Galileo Galilei in the development of the microscope. This is a work of restrained tenderness that in style, subject, and treatment of artificial light also suggests a debt to the scientific-figure paintings of Joseph Wright of Derby, whose orrery and air-pump pictures were well known through engravings.

Weir was one of a number of mid-19th-century artists best known for their role as history painters. Historical art of the 19th century has fallen into disrepute, however, and thus specialists in this form have followed it into relative obscurity, though there will probably be an inevitable rediscovery of both the art and the artists. Unlike such a landscape painter as Tilton, however, these artists have usually left behind isolated historical monuments of substantial size — Weir's painting in the Capitol is such an example — so that they are not totally forgotten. Furthermore, a number of them were also prominent teachers, and therefore are still remembered today in that capacity. *History painters*

Another such painter was Christian Schussele. He was born in Alsace and studied in Strasbourg and then in Paris. In the latter city he became a chromolithographer, an art which he practiced in Philadelphia when he immigrated in 1848. In 1854 he successfully established himself as a history painter and went on to become an important figure in Philadelphia art life, serving as the first Professor of Drawing and Painting at the Pennsylvania Academy of the Fine Arts, from 1868 until his death.

Since historical painters must inevitably become adept at both individual figure construction and the manipulation of groups, the lighter and more popular theme of genre also often engaged such artists' attention, and it is such works by Schussele that find a warmer reception today. Even some of these are loaded with a kind of pathetic sentiment and morality that appears very heavy handed; but others are marked by a light and gay spirit, such as *The Young Recruits,* 1855 (cat. no. 35). Schussele's training in French academic circles is evident — like Boisseau, Schussele, was a pupil of Delaroche — but here it is coupled with the influence of Dusseldorf realism in the concentration upon the contrasting ages of the figures, the differentiation of types and the plethora of incident.

Traces of early social realism

One of the best-known painters of history and religious pictures of his time, yet mentioned only in passing in art history books today, is Thomas Pritchard Rossiter. He was a New York painter, an intimate of Asher B. Durand and John F. Kensett. Like Schussele, he, too, occasionally painted genre pictures, but his involved social commentary and even satire. Two works painted in 1857, the *City* and *Rural Post Office,* involve the postal system, a subject that attracted our genre artists. Such popularity was owing in part to the system's development at that time, and in part to the opportunity it gave the artist to contrast great crowds of people of different ages, physiognomy, and social status. It also, of course, is another example of the period's fascination with the "news," for news is certainly what the postal service delivered; and the artists who painted this theme concentrated on the different reactions of the receivers of letters. But Rossiter's pictures, being paired, allowed the artist to emphasize still another favorite consideration in American genre — the idyllic atmosphere of the rural post office in contrast with the more frenzied, troubled, and class-distinct city post office.

Rossiter's *Such is Life, A Scene in London During the Crimean War* (cat. no. 34), is an English scene painted by an American artist in Paris in 1855, where Rossiter had gone two years earlier. It reveals aspects of all three countries. The social satire is worthy of Daumier, though it is depicted with almost Pre-Raphaelite color and detail. Rossiter condemns British class distinctions, contrasting the smug, superior wealthy ladies, the obtuse military, and the condescending clergy with the pathetic poverty of the poor, whether bereaved widows or starving matchboys. An animal equivalent is seen in the pugnacious bulldog and the ratty mongrel. "Social Realism" — a quality seldom found in American painting of the time but sanctioned in this work because it condemns the national follies of a *foreign* country — is embodied in the topical aspect of the picture. While economic distinctions of vast magnitude, crime, and strife are rampant, the nation's leaders are oblivious to the further hardships imposed by involvement in foreign warfare. Trainloads of soldiers depart for the front, while others return crippled, maimed, or dead.

Weir, Schussele and Rossiter were in their own time best-known for historical pictures. Another practitioner of grand-manner painting was Thomas Buchanan Read. He was first encouraged by Washington Allston, in Boston, whom he met in 1841 and who had directed such notable artists as Samuel F. B. Morse, Horatio Greenough, William Page, and William Rimmer toward the ideal in art. Read, who had started his artistic career in Cincinnati under the patronage of Nicholas Longworth, made his first trip to Europe in 1850, where he was one of the earliest American artists to be associated with the young Pre-Raphaelite painters; he became a friend of Dante Gabriel Rossetti. If all this did not provide him with sufficient background for the pursuit of historical painting, further encouragement must surely have come from a visit with Emanuel Leutze, then working in Düsseldorf on his *Washington Crossing the Delaware.*

Read returned to Philadelphia in 1852, but America could not keep him long. He was soon back in Europe, this time in Italy and especially Florence. There he associated with a group of American sculptors and with the literary circle, including the Brownings. The death of his first wife drew him back to America; but upon his remarriage the following year, he returned to Italy, this time to Rome. He remained in Italy, except for serving the Union during the Civil War, until shortly before his death in 1872.

Like the American sculptors working in Florence and Rome, Read and a number of other American painters found the cultural climate of Italy far more congenial to the practice of ideal art than mid-century America. Along with the landscape painters already mentioned, these artists enjoyed the patronage of visiting Americans, but they were free to develop their art in a way that was not possible in mercantile New York, Philadelphia, and Boston; like those landscape painters, also, many expatriate grand-manner artists subsequently fell into oblivion, having maintained only tenuous connections with the contemporary art community back in America. Read achieved greater fame during his lifetime as a poet than as an artist. He is still remembered for his poem "Sheridan's Ride," but he is less remembered for his many paintings of the same subject.

Read painted a number of religious subjects, but these and most of his other ideal paintings were more fanciful than dramatic, more concerned with ethereal grace than the stern moralizing advocated by his Pre-Raphaelite contemporaries or by Leutze in his history pieces. Because Read's closest companions among artists were the American sculptors in Florence and Rome, it is not surprising that his subjects were often similar to theirs – *Undine, Prosperine,* the *Culprit Fay,* the *Lost Pleiad,* and fairies, spirits, and the like. The contemporary landscape painter Sanford Gifford described Read's subject matter as "mostly scenes in Fairy Land," and Nathanial Hawthorne alluded to Read in *The Marble Faun*: "...we might indicate a poet-painter, whose song has the vividness of picture, and whose canvas is peopled with angels, fairies, and watersprites, one to the ethereal life, because he saw them face to face in his poetic mood." Read lived in Rome at 53 Via Margutta, and in the same building or near him were the sculptors Randolph Rogers, Joseph Mozier, Chauncey B. Ives, William Henry Rinehart, and Margaret Foley; the last named sculpted a bust of Read's wife.

One of the most romantic of Read's idyls is *A Painter's Dream,* 1869 (cat. no. 32), a view of the artist lost in a reverie of ideal feminine beauty with cupids or angels in attendance. Read's painting is a true example of visionary art, a Victorian compromise of sensuality with innocence. It is a vision we know better from contemporary American sculpture, but in painting it was presented and kept alive at the mid-century by only a handful of artists, most of whom worked in Rome for much of their careers.

Animal images in genre painting

Two mid-century genre painters of particular note are the brothers James Henry Beard and William Holbrook Beard. James, the older, is a particularly significant figure in the development of genre, but both artists deserve far greater respect than they are presently given. James Beard's early genre paintings stand peculiarly between those of Mount and Bingham — midway, so to speak, in subject matter, technique, and even chronology and geography (Mount lived in New York State and died in 1868 and Bingham settled in Missouri and died in 1879, Beard was active in Cincinnati between 1834 and 1870). His early genre paintings have a quietly humorous character, but a number of his later ones emanate a strong social consciousness almost unique for the period. However, some-time before moving to New York City in 1870, Beard changed the empha-sis of his art to the depiction of animals, a theme which also became the specialty of his younger brother William. His brother was also a portrait-ist, and only further study will reveal which of the two adopted animal subject matter first and if one influenced the other. The Beards became the finest animal painters in America, though the art has often been accused of "vulgarity." They frequently used animal images to portray the follies and weaknesses of humanity; and neither was above painting pictures that were ribald and raucus, for the allegorical substitution of animal for human allowed them to depict improprieties otherwise not permitted in Victorian art and society.

Though the Beard brothers both specialized in "animal moralities" their art was quite distinct. James tended to paint domestic animals, William, wilder ones. James's animals were often viewed up close, and placed in interior settings amid furniture and draperies and other acces-sories that suggest his background in genre. William usually placed his animals in outdoor settings; his best-known works are two huge canvases of the bulls and bears (literally) of Wall Street, although he also painted several lovely pure landscapes. He was a sculptor, as well, and prepared sculptural renditions of animals from which he painted his pictures; in 1870 he also prepared an amazing design for a museum of art to be erected in Central Park and entered through a series of underground pass-ageways or grottoes, these lined with enormous sculptures of — animals.

The works by the two Beards in this exhibition are typical of their individual styles, and are masterworks of their kind. James's *The Parson's Pets,* 1874 (cat. no. 4), was well-known in his own time. The complex combination of animals, their wild destructiveness and savage humor, the brilliant tonalities of the creatures, were never surpassed by him. William's *Susannah and the Elders,* 1865 (cat. no. 5), is a parody of the famous religious theme undertaken by so many of the Old Masters from Peter Paul Rubens and Titian on; only here the lovely lady is replaced by a graceful swan and the two old lechers are glowering owls. It is satirical and witty, but it is also lovely — the animals beautifully rendered, the landscape verdant and beckoning, the forms softer and more integrated than the sharply linear work by James.

The history of American sculpture differs in many respects from that of painting, reflecting, perhaps its much later start. Professional sculptors only appeared at the beginning of the 19th century, and indeed a professional school of sculptors really originated with those artists who began to live in Italy – Florence and Rome – in 1825. These expatriates, working in Italy, were patronized primarily by Americans, though also by the English, Italians and Russians; they dominated the artistic scene until the Philadelphia Centennial, a period of roughly fifty years or two generations. Their home was Italy, their medium was marble, and their aesthetic was the re-creation of the forms and formal ideals of the classical world, though with an overlay of Christian morality and Victorian sentimentality which led critics to deem their works superior in moral content to the hallowed art of antiquity.

American sculpture

These artists produced both portraits and "ideal" works. Most considered their portrait sculptures potboilers, and their ideal works their major efforts. Most were men, but not all; and the most surprising fact about the American sculpture colony in Rome was that a large number of women were active in it. Henry James referred to them as the "white marmorean flock," women who exercised an American freedom by adopting a profession into which women had rarely entered before – though there were such precedents as the English artist of the late 18th century, Anne Seymour Damer, and the contemporary French woman painter and sculptor, Rosa Bonheur.

Women sculptors

American independence, yes, but perhaps it was more safely expressed among Rome's Pincian Hills, far from the watchful and possibly disapproving eyes of still puritanical America. The group centered on Charlotte Cushman, a famous actress and lecturer who spent a great deal of time in Rome. The first of her charges whom she escorted to Europe in 1852, and the American woman sculptor who was probably the most talented and would achieve the greatest fame of all was Harriet Hosmer. She studied in Rome with the major English neoclassicist, John Gibson. This tutelage was particularly valuable in providing her not only with the best possible training in the neoclassic style but with English contacts, often among the wealthy, collecting nobility, so that Harriet Hosmer became equally well-known in England and America. Her drift into an English ambiance, coupled with the sculptor's predilection for literary subject matter, brought her into contact and friendship with the poets Elizabeth Barrett and William Browning, who were living in Italy. In the winter of 1853 this friendship led Harriet to sculpt and cast the *Hands of Robert and Elizabeth Browning* (cat. no. 22), one of the most personal and moving sculptures by a member of this group of American artists. Touchingly affecting in the contrast between Elizabeth's frailness and the strong grasp of her husband, it is a monument to their "togetherness." On Elizabeth's death, in 1861, Harriet wrote these moving, and appropriate lines:

"Parted by death," we say,
Yet, "hand in hand they went their eternal way."

The sculpture was described by Hawthorne in *The Marble Faun*, and though Harriet Hosmer created several more famous works, such as *Puck, Beatrice Cenci,* and the monumental *Zenobia,* none was so intimate or heartfelt as this.

Harriet Hosmer may be neglected, but she is hardly forgotten. Edward R. Thaxter is scarcely remembered at all. He is possibly a relative of the poetess, Celia Thaxter, whose home on the island of Appledore in the Isles of Shoals was to provide inspiration and retreat for such late-19th-century artists as Childe Hassam. An expatriate, Thaxter died in Italy at twenty-seven, too young to have achieved more than the briefest of recognition, and he quickly fell into obscurity. Yet he was an artist of tremendous power. The violent expressiveness of *The Fury,* 1881 (cat. no. 39), is superior to that of any of his contemporaries or artistic forebearers in this country, with the possible exception of William Rimmer (one wonders if Thaxter had been a pupil of Rimmer at the School of the Museum of Fine Arts in Boston). *The Fury,* created in the year of Thaxter's death, embodies an uncontrolled rushing movement, and has a baroque intensity which imbued even some of the more traditional, "controlled" examples of neoclassicism, such as Randolph Rogers's *Nydia;* but nothing produced by those expatriate artists has the force and vigor of this head.

The Fury may be the unlocated bust by Thaxter of *Meg Merrilies,* a character in Sir Walter Scott's novel, *Guy Mannering,* for Scott's description of her tallies closely with the appearance of this work: "(She was) full six feet high, ...rather masculine than feminine. Her dark elf-locks shot out like snakes of the gorgon, ...heightening the singular effect of her strong and weather-beaten features, ...while her eye had a wild roll that indicated something like real or affected insanity."

The American reaction to neoclassicism

The reaction to the dominance of neoclassicism in American sculpture began even during the height of that movement, for it was denounced as an alien art form, derived from Europe and Antiquity, with little or no relevance to the American experience. Thaxter's personal expressionism was one form of reaction; another was a new realism in American sculpture, whether expressed in the good-humored, popular plaster genre groups of John Rogers, the monumentally naturalistic bronze sculptures of John Quincy Adams Ward and others, or the more intimate realism of such a painter-sculptor as Thomas Eakins. Eakins's favorite pupil, in turn, was Samuel Murray, who in 1887 studied at the Art Students League of Philadelphia, that short-lived teaching organization formed by students protesting Eakins's dismissal as director of the Pennsylvania Academy, where he had succeeded Christian Schussele. Murray worked with Eakins and shared his studio for over ten years. The League had been formed with the study of the nude as its basis — partly in defiance of the reactionary academy schools. Although Murray studied sculpture under Eakins, the two men later collaborated in creating sculpture. Murray introduced Eakins to hitherto unknown elements of everyday Philadelphia life, particularly the world of prize fighting, which Eakins was to depict in several monumental canvases in 1898 and '99, including *Salutat* and *Between Rounds.* At the same time, Murray created his bronze *Boxer,* 1899 (cat. no. 31). The figure appears to be Billy Smith, the prize fighter who was the subject of the two Eakins pictures just named. The Murray sculpture embodies Eakins's understanding and respect for the expressive powers of the human form, and it is a testimonial to a friendship that was significant in the development of late-19th-century American art.

Despite the human scale of the Murray *Boxer,* the major thrust of American sculpture of the time was a movement toward monumental realism combined with a new regard for Renaissance traditions. It is best known through the works created at the turn of the century by Augustus Saint-Gaudens and Daniel Chester French. The third in a trio of leading sculptors of the period was Frederick MacMonnies, who had been a student of Saint-Gaudens. Advised by the latter to pursue painting as well as sculpture, MacMonnies went to Paris armed with letters to John Singer Sargent and Paul Baudry, as well as to the sculptor Jean Alexandre Falguière. MacMonnies primarily pursued the sculptor's career, but his vacillation between the two mediums never ceased; even on his first trip to Europe he studied painting in Munich. As a sculptor, MacMonnies is not, of course, a neglected master; his figures, from the gigantic *Triumph of Columbia* erected at the Chicago World's Columbian Exposition of 1893, to his statue of *Nathan Hale* in New York's City Hall Park and his dancing *Bacchante with Infant Faun,* at The Metropolitan Museum of Art, are extremely well known. But, as a painter, he is almost totally neglected.

In his early years, he gave much time to painting, and an exhibition in New York City in 1903 at the Durand-Ruel Galleries featured works in both mediums. He painted as well as taught sculpture in the studio-school he founded at Giverny outside of Paris in 1905; and Giverny, of course, was famous as a painter's colony with French and American painters such as Claude Monet and Theodore Robinson. Furthermore, MacMonnies's wife, Mary Fairchild, was also a painter.

MacMonnies's sculpture differs from that of Saint-Gaudens and French in its painterliness. His bronze figures have undulating surfaces that glitter in the light, broken outlines and a sense of tremulous movement that is unlike the more glyptic treatment of, for example, Saint-Gaudens. His painting — like his sculpture — is also "painterly"; he is concerned with brushwork, lightness, and the capture of a moment more inherent in painting than in sculpture. These qualities abound in his beautiful *Portrait of the Artist* (cat. no. 28), probably painted in the early years of the 20th century in Europe. He sees himself quite objectively yet trenchantly; the elegant, aristocratic, and upright, bearing of the figure and the general semi-Impressionist treatment suggest that he found inspiration in Velasquez. There is confirmation of this suggestion in the background painting, Velasquez's *Topers* in the Prado. One of a number MacMonnies copied in the Prado in 1898, the Velasquez also becomes a strong compositional foil. Its strongly articulated frame establishes a geometric structure and prohibits the eye from traveling backward, while its basic horizontal shape balances the erect verticality of MacMonnies's own figure. The darkness of the Baroque canvas strongly silhouettes the brilliantly lit face of the artist himself. The scintillating brushwork, the lightness and painterly quality, all suggest MacMonnies deserves a place equivalent to the better-known portrait artists of his time, Sargent, Giovanni Boldini, and others.

Thematically, the most significant development in late-19th-century American art was the emergence of figure painting as the major vehicle for aesthetic communication. The figure was used for emotional expression, divorced from specific portraiture or often even from anecdotal purpose. Such a development is intimately allied with the new migration of American art students to Paris and Munich, where the study of the figure was the heritage of strong academic emphasis dating back to neoclassic times.

American artists not only studied in Paris under the leading academic painters, either in specific ateliers or at the Ecole des Beaux-Arts, they also attempted, often successfully, to rival the contemporary French masters by exhibiting in the Paris salons. Their subject matter often paralleled that of their European colleagues: paintings of Norman and Breton peasants; costume pieces of the 17th and 18th centuries; less often, exotic and sensual paintings of the nude; and occasionally, monumental and dramatic classical scenes. Among the American painters creating monumental pictures for the Salons were two women — Elizabeth Gardner, who studied under William Bouguereau and later married him, and Sarah Paxton Ball Dodson, whose *The Bacidae,* 1883 (cat. no. 18), is shown here. Miss Dodson studied first in her native city, Philadelphia, with Christian Schussele at the Pennsylvania Academy. There she may have discovered a penchant for history painting, one which was certainly furthered when she moved to Paris to study with Jules Lefebvre. She began exhibiting at the Paris Salon in 1877, showing pictures not unlike *The Bacidae,* where a full-scale depiction of the nude is combined with dramatic gesture in an oracular subject. Sarah Dodson occasionally depicted scenes relating to the history of her native land, but she was essentially an expatriate; the later part of her life was spent in England, in London and Brighton.

Academic figure painting was practiced in the United States by such artists as Abbott Thayer and George de Forest Brush. The former specialized in depictions of young, virginal women; the latter, in more mature figures, but the work of both is tinged with a kind of poetic, idealistic melancholy. The central figures of these Brush paintings, whether identified as "mother and child" or "Mother and Child," are in effect updatings of the Renaissance religious image. Indeed, the Renaissance revival, which strongly influenced both contemporary American architectural forms and the sculpture of such well-known masters as Saint-Gaudens and French, found its most ardent interpreter among the painters in Brush; this reflection of Italian Renaissance art is further emphasized in the frames in which his paintings of mothers and children are often encased. The divorce from day-to-day reality and contemporary themes, the retreat into the ideal, the reflection of such masters as Botticelli in his work suggest a parallel with the Symbolist world of the late-19th-century and turn-of-the-century in Europe, without, in Brush's case, the elements of decadence which infuse much Symbolist painting. Brush's career witnessed equal emphasis upon his poetic, secular Madonnas and Indian subject matter, at once ethnologically accurate and yet romantic and idealized.

American Art Nouveau   In Europe, Symbolism merged with and in a sense was replaced by Art Nouveau. This artistic form was primarily in evidence in architecture and the decorative and applied arts; its reflection in painting and sculpture seems much more limited and tangential. The American masterwork of Art Nouveau painting is undoubtedly John White Alexander's *Isabella and the Pot of Basil,* 1897 (cat. no. 1), based on a morbid story taken from Boccaccio but best known in Keats's famous poem "Isabella; or The Pot

32

of Basil." To understand Art Nouveau pictorial imagery, one need only compare Alexander's treatment of this theme with William Holman Hunt's Pre-Raphaelite version of the subject. In the present work, the languid voluptuousness, abstract linear rhythms, billowing forms, and eerie lighting of the demented Isabella as she sensually caresses the large pot containing her lover's severed head, replaces the intensity of expression and detailed historicism of the Hunt.

Alexander studied abroad, not in Paris but in Munich, the center to which so many young American art students gravitated in the 1870s; he worked there and at Polling in Bavaria, where the famous Munich-American, Frank Duveneck, had started to teach, and others, such as J. Frank Currier, lived much of their lives. Alexander, however, began to incorporate Art Nouveau forms into his art in Paris at the turn of the century. Aspects of this style can be found in many of the portraits he painted in America, as well as in his poetic figure paintings, often with floral titles taken from attributes in the paintings. Here his Isabella is accompanied by several blossoms which almost literally add an odor of decadence. All of Alexander's figure paintings and portraits are competent and individual, but none offers such an intense expression as the present one; he was also an illustrator of distinction and a noted muralist.

The exodus of large numbers of American artists for Munich began in the 1860s, although the most famous of these artists are noted for their study there a decade later. Among the latter was Carl von Marr, an artist whose reputation, although high in its own time, has greatly declined. He is mainly remembered in his native city, Milwaukee, where he is usually considered the most significant Wisconsin painter of the 19th century. When in his twenties, Marr went to Munich, and unlike Duveneck, Alexander, William Merritt Chase, Walter Shirlaw, Robert Blum, and a host of others, he remained there. Thus, Marr's art is not only very much a part of late-19th-century German painting, it has been virtually forgotten in his native land. This is, however, an injustice to him. He made voyages back to America and painted here to; many of his pictures were noticed and discussed in America at the end of the 19th century, and a number of his major works are in American collections, private and public. The present work, *Christmas Eve,* 1884 (cat. no. 42), was painted in response to a feeling of homesickness; the darkness of the picture reflects the dramatic chiaroscuro which marks much Munich painting of the period, but an interest in light and color appears to be characteristic of Marr's work, especially his less ambitious and historical pieces.

American artists in Munich

Another Munich painter was the New York-born Louis Charles Moeller. Moeller studied in Munich with the German artist, Wilhelm Diez, and with Frank Duveneck, but his art did not reflect the broad, free brushwork and the dramatic chiaroscuro of Duveneck's. Back home, Moeller established both a style and a subject matter of his own. He painted genre scenes, but more often semi-portraits — interior scenes with actual persons, usually two or more together, engaged in everyday activities. The rooms which they occupy are usually those of the well-to-do, and are often claustrophobic in the accumulation of bric-a-brac. Moeller's paintings are somewhat reminiscent of the German and Austrian still lifes popular in Munich at the time — by artists such as Camilla Friedländer and others. His coloration is usually dark and rich, his forms rather solid and "blocky," his figures plastic and geometric, which together make Moeller's paintings easily identifiable.

His *Sculptor's Studio* (cat. no. 30) is at once extremely unusual and very beautiful. The attention to detail, the incorporation of manifold objects, is characteristic; but the openness, the sense of light and atmosphere, and the tonalities are all unique. Above all, the absence of figures is both unusual and provocative. It is by inference an autobiographical painting. Moeller here tells of an artist's way of life, his interests and aspirations — perhaps his own. The painting of an artist's studio, of course, is not unusual — many artists have depicted themselves and their colleagues in studio interiors, and the subject calls to mind such diverse examples as those by Rembrandt or, closer to home, by the 19th-century artist William Sidney Mount.

Although the depiction of the empty studio is less common, it has precedents in the painting of empty rooms, and this tradition appears to be primarily German. In the early 19th century, for example, there are partial room interiors, unpeopled, by Caspar David Friedrich and his school, though these usually center on open windows and suggest a desire to communicate with the infinite and the unknowable. Closer to Moeller's in conception and date is the Berlin artist, Adolf von Menzel's 1845 *Room with a Balcony,* though it is freer and more painterly; though not a studio picture, it too is autobiographical: a view of the Menzel family apartment. Menzel's painting is at once more elegant and more anonymous than Moeller's, which directs us specifically to an artist; and it is rather like the well-known rococo interiors, devoid of figures, which became the speciality of the American artist, Walter Gay. Moeller's picture also has some parallels in the 1879 painting by George Bacon Wood, *Interior of the Library of the Late Henry Carey,* a picture in which art abounds. That is, truly, a memorial picture, made eloquent by the rich accumulation of possessions by the subject, whose departure from life is symbolized by the lack of any human presence. Such paintings of empty interiors are rare but extremely effective pictures.

From Cincinnati to Munich

Munich and Paris were equally popular in the late 19th century among American art students, and some, of course, studied in both; though eventually Paris was the undisputed center for foreign study. Of all major American cities, Cincinnati in particular continued to supply large numbers of young Americans for the academies and the ateliers in Munich, undoubtedly because of the large German immigration to that city at the mid-century. In other words, these young Americans were returning to the national origin of their heritage.

Duveneck was one of these Cincinnati artists, of course, and many of the others studied or worked with him in Munich. One of these was Henry F. Farny, who was born in Alsace but grew up in the Middle Western United States. He had gone to Europe in the late 1860s, where he was befriended by Thomas Buchanan Read, also represented in this exhibition, and worked in Düsseldorf. But his major training took place in Munich with Duveneck and under Duveneck's friend, Wilhelm Diez.

Farny returned to Cincinnati, but while his artistic style was formed in Europe, his primary subject matter was discovered on voyages to the American West. Farny not only became the one major Cincinnati painter to investigate the Indian subject, he was probably the finest painter of the

Indian in the late 19th century. His relative obscurity — except in Cincinnati, where his work is much prized — is perhaps owing to its lack of flamboyance. Farny was a contemporary of Frederic Remington and Charles Russell, but his work lacks the dramatic flair, flaming colors, and great emphasis upon action of their art. Nor is his light as brilliant; and his work, unlike theirs, is usually quite small. But there is a keen understanding of figural construction, the manipulation of space, and the integration of the figure with the landscape that is missing in the painting of his more celebrated contemporaries. Forms and color are cool and crisp. Farny was an accurate ethnologist, but he was also a consummate artist; and his painting transcended the reportorial, illustrational nature of Remington's and Russell's art.

Of all the American artists in Munich who achieved fame in their own day, Walter Shirlaw is probably the most forgotten today. He was of Scottish birth but grew up in New York City, where he remained until he went to Europe in 1870. He arrived in Paris, but he spent most of his seven years abroad in Munich, and was usually considered, along with Duveneck and Chase, a leading American artist in that city. He returned to New York to become the first professor at the newly formed Art Students League and one of the founders of the Society of American Artists, which in the early days of this progressive new organization had a large Munich representation. Shirlaw also participated in the revival of mural decoration at the end of the century, and investigated the stained-glass medium.

The *Waterlilies* (cat. no. 37) must have been painted in the 1870s, for *The American nude* it was exhibited at the Brooklyn Institute in 1879. The Munich painters, like their Parisian contemporaries, were devoted to the painting of the human figure, either nude or clothed, and Shirlaw painted a large number of idyllic studies of the nude. In the late 19th century, the nude was usually depicted in an outdoor setting, often in a water environment, which thus provided a naturalistic raison d'être, and further, a symbolic suggestion of cleanliness to counter any objections of impurity. Often, particularly in American art, the figures discreetly turned their backs toward the spectator, and the painting gained further acceptability through the assignment of appealing titles — frequently floral in nature, thus uniting "flora" and "fauna" within the painting. Such is the character of this, one of the finest of Shirlaw's known ventures into nude subject matter. The figures are treated informally, befitting their unselfconscious nature, and yet they have vague classical reference to such traditionally acceptable subjects as the Three Graces and the Judgment of Paris. The figure construction is somewhat more painterly and dramatic than one might find in the work of Parisian and Parisian-trained artists, and is typical of the Munich tradition of which Shirlaw was very much a part.

Younger than Shirlaw, or his fellow Cincinnatian, Farny, was Robert *Venice in the 1880s* Blum, the son of well-to-do members of the German community in that city. Although he may have studied in Munich on his own, he never studied at the academy there; rather, he is associated with Duveneck during the latter's stay in Venice in 1880, where Duveneck and the "Duveneck boys" were working, along with James McNeill Whistler. Blum's involvement with both etching and pastel most probably derives from his association with Whistler at that time.

The other important result of Blum's trip was a fascination and love for the city of Venice itself. Venice, indeed, captured the imagination of many American artists in the late 19th century — earlier, it had been somewhat bypassed for Florence, Rome, and even Naples — but its unique setting and the water, light, and atmosphere attracted many American artists from the 1870s on. Blum was one of these; during the 1880s he visited Venice almost every year. His most important easel paintings are depictions of Venice, either canal scenes or figure pictures. Of the latter, two are outstanding: *Venetian Lace Makers,* of 1885-87, the better known, and its sequel, *The Italian Bead Stringers* (cat. no. 6). The *Bead Stringers* was painted in Venice in 1887-88, but the *Lace Makers* was begun in Venice and finished back in America; the delay owing to the difficulty of working without the original models.

The two pictures are companion works, painted at the same time and involving women handworkers in Venice. They contrast also; one is an indoor scene, the other, an outdoor courtyard; thus they present contrasting problems of light and of painting the figure in direct versus indirect sunlight. The combination in the *Bead Stringers* of solid figural construction with scintillating brushwork and an interest in light is evidence of the influence of a Spanish painter who worked in Italy, Mariano Fortuny. Although Fortuny is not a household word anymore, in the late 19th century he was a famous if tragically short-lived artist of tremendous influence, and one much patronized by wealthy Americans. Admiration for Fortuny's art came from both patrons and artists, and his influence was felt by no one so much as Blum, who was nicknamed "Blumtuny."

In 1890, Blum went to Japan, arriving at the same time as John La Farge, and was one of the first Americans there. He was joined by his good friend Charles Ulrich, in whose Venetian studio he had painted the *Bead Stringers.* On his return, Blum was involved with the Mendelssohn Hall murals, now at The Brooklyn Museum, and later with murals for New York's New Amsterdam Theater, before his early death by pneumonia.

Although Blum was not strictly one of the Munich painters, he was certainly in their ambiance; he knew almost all of them and was a good friend of Chase, Duveneck, and others. The *French Cottage,* 1883 (cat. no. 2), by Abraham Archibald Anderson appears almost Chaselike in its use of light, color, and paint, a kind of limited Impressionism. Yet, he was involved neither with the progressive Munich artists nor with the French or the American Impressionists, and Anderson's best-known works in his own time — he is almost totally forgotten today — were oriental genre scenes, in the tradition of Gérôme or of the American, Frederic Bridgman, and later, official portraits. Anderson's training was with the academic French artist, Léon Bonnat, and he was a frequent exhibitor in the Paris Salons, dividing his time between Paris and New York. The present picture, then, is indicative of the freedom and progressive nature of the more informal work of even "official" and academic artists of the late 19th century.

French Impressionism and its effect on American painting

In late-19th-century American art, the dark drama of Munich gave way to the brilliant light and color of Impressionism. French Impressionist painting was first introduced into America on a large scale in 1886, although individual examples of such work had been seen here previously, and certain patrons and artists traveling and working abroad knew of

Impressionist developments much earlier. American identification
with the movement was also recognized early; in 1883 works by John
Twachtman and William Gedney Bunce were termed "examples of the
impressionist school," while in 1886 an article appeared entitled
"Whistler, the Head of the Impressionists." Nor was this appellation in-
correct, for the contact between Whistler and the Duveneck boys in
Venice in 1880-81 appears to have been crucial for the early introduction
of Impressionism into America, particularly through the more sketchy and
at the same time more acceptable medium of pastel, which was enthusias-
tically adopted by American artists in the 1880s and much patronized too.
The lighter tonality, freer technique, greater colorism inherent in pastel
seem to have prepared the way for the acceptance of, and even strong
positive support for, Impressionist oil painting by the early 1890s.

Not that there were no critics of Impressionism in America, just as
there were also in France, but here the criticism seems to have been less
intense, more muted. Samuel Benjamin in 1880 criticized Impressionism
as trying to represent the soul without the body, and George Inness published strong condemnation of the movement in the 1880s, though he
himself had been called a "colorist" and a "luminarist" in the previous
decade and had been criticized for having sacrificed form and structure
for color. Yet, acute change can be seen not only year by year but almost
month by month in the early 1890s, and the Chicago World's Columbian
Exposition of 1893 seems to have sanctified Impressionism in America.

The reasons for its early acceptance in this country are many and
complex: certainly the lack of a strong academic tradition, against which
Impressionism was a reaction, is important. Also, Impressionism took on
poetic and decorative overtones, and American Impressionists often com-
promised Impressionist tenets with traditional realist tendencies, as well as
with the more low-key tonalist art growing out of Inness's later works,
already accepted and admired in America. Subsequently, this tendency
toward compromise in a movement that was also seen as derivative from
French painting led to a disdain for much American Impressionism,
though such painting has regained admirers in recent years.

In the 1880s there were a number of American artists whose painting
provided a transition from *plein-air* landscape to full-blown Impressionism.
Naturally enough, these artists, in effect expatriates, were strongly cogni-
zant of French Impressionism. The little-known Mark Fisher may actually
have been the first American Impressionist; his mature career was spent
entirely in England. Mary Cassatt's importance to Impressionism in
America cannot be overestimated, not only because of her own work but
also because she actively championed the collecting of Impressionist painting by wealthy Americans whom she guided. John Singer Sargent figures
here, too, particularly with regard to his outdoor landscape and figure
painting produced while working in England in the late 1880s, at Broad-
way and Calcott.

Sargent, in turn, had a strong influence at the time upon Dennis
Miller Bunker, a fine Boston painter. Bunker, a superb portraitist and
sensitive landscape painter, was tragically short-lived; but in the 1880s,
which encompass his entire maturity, he was highly thought of and much
patronized in Boston, and he had a strong influence upon other Boston
painters. Crucial to the development of his late landscape style was the

summer of 1888 which he spent with Sargent at Calcott; Sargent's semi-Impressionist technique in *plein-air* landscape painting, emphasizing strong sunlight achieved by quill-like brushstrokes, was adopted by Bunker and applied to the vibrant green and yellow landscapes he painted the following summers of 1889 and 1890 in Medfield, Massachusetts (such as *The Pool, Medfield,* 1889 (cat. no. 12). Bunker was intensely sensitive to the appearance of nature on different days, and depicted seemingly uncomposed areas of nature, with long diagonals into space emphasizing a sense of depth. His paintings were airy, and light, with brushstrokes like "fish-hooks," according to Edmund Tarbell, his Boston contemporary.

Bunker's art is not only beautiful and sensitive in its own right, but it had an important place in transmitting Impressionist principles and techniques to American artists. By the end of the decade following Bunker's death in 1890, Impressionism was so enshrined in America that there developed in 1898 a group called "The Ten American Painters," described subsequently as a sort of academy of American Impressionism. Some of the artists of "The Ten" are today extremely well known, men such as Childe Hassam, Theodore Robinson, John Twachtman, and William Merritt Chase. The work of others of the group has yet to be revived, particularly the artists more involved with the figure than with landscape. One of the most original of "The Ten" was Robert Reid, who worked out of an enormous New York studio jokingly called the "Golf Links"! Reid is often thought of as a decorative Impressionist, presenting the figures of lovely young women in swirling costumes, combined with floral elements and still lifes. There is an overall patterning and rather flattened composition in Reid's pictures that also made his style pertinent for his work in mural decoration and stained glass. Reid's work, however, is more than just decorative; in its concern with pattern it is allied with the contemporary French painting of such Post-Impressionists as Pierre Bonnard and Edouard Vuillard, while its serpentine linear rhythms are closer to Art Nouveau stylization.

Square format in painting

Boston was particularly sympathetic to Impressionism, particularly in its more gentle and more aristocratic form, emphasizing the depiction of elegant women in repose in light-filled landscapes. Some of these Boston painters, such as Edmund Tarbell and Frank Benson, are well-known today and particularly well respected there. Others, such as Edward Wilbur Dean Hamilton, are scarcely recalled. That often-found American combination of Impressionist light and color with a sense of the solid reality of material forms is present in *Summer at Campobello, New Brunswick,* ca. 1890-1900 (cat. no. 20), as is a structured illusionism of space. An interesting aspect of this painting is its square format; square paintings are not uncommon in American art from 1880 on, first in the art of Albert Pinkham Ryder and then among the American Impressionists, particularly Twachtman and Willard Metcalf. There is a very conscious and purposeful choice on the part of artists who adopt the square format and a very anti-traditional one. It was investigated by numerous Americans at the end of the 19th century, including Winslow Homer, and was adopted by Marsden Hartley for many of his early Maine landscapes, which is not surprising considering his respect for the art of Ryder and Twachtman. The meaning of the square format is too complex to be developed here, but it relates to a very modern conception of keeping the forms depicted within a closed framework and upon the surface of the painting; thus it is an early step toward the discarding of traditional illusionism. Although Hamilton's painting is more traditional than the abstracted works of Ryder, Twachtman, and even the square pictures of Homer and Hassam, it reveals this little-known, delightful painter as an artist concerned with a number of the progressive aesthetic concerns of his day.

Full-blown Impressionism, à la Monet, is best represented here by the painting *Cornshucks and Windmill,* 1909 (cat. no. 41), by Allen Tucker. Since Tucker studied with Twachtman, his interest in Impressionist light, color, and brushwork is not surprising. His truly Impressionist period, however, and perhaps his most sensitive painting, was of brief duration, for he became absorbed with the expressive forms of Post-Impressionism and especially the art of Vincent van Gogh; his later work consists of not unattractive pastiches of that great modern master's work. But the vibrant colorism, the dissolution of form, the overall excited brushwork in commalike strokes, and the colored shadows and omission of blacks and grays mark the present work as one of the truest examples of American Impressionism; indeed, the subject, cornshucks, becomes a sort of American-idiom counterpart to the haystacks of Claude Monet.

Walter Gay has been previously mentioned for his specialization in empty, elegant room interiors, usually of the rococo period in France. Gay painted these works in France where he lived for more than sixty years, and was an associate of other more famous Americans living abroad, such as Henry James, Mary Cassatt, James Abbott McNeill Whistler, and John Singer Sargent. Gay had begun his career in Boston, however, and at first was a floral painter, working in a free, painterly manner. *Wild Flowers,* 1875 (cat. no. 18), is a notable example of his work in that period. He was one of a group of artists, such as Albion Bicknell and William Babcock, who had abandoned the tight, scientific manner of the mid-century and devoted themselves to more poetic and expressive renditions of their floral subjects, but only the flower paintings of John La Farge are well known today. James Jackson Jarves noted and approved the change from botany to poetry in flower painting when he wrote that La Farge's floral pictures "are as tender and true suggestions of flowers – not copies – as nature ever grew, and affect our senses in the same delightful way. Their language is of the heart and they talk to us of human love and God's goodness. ... We bear away from the sight of them in our inmost souls, new and joyful utterances of nature."

The poetic and lyric approach to still life is one of several departures from that mid-century emphasis on scientific botany and optimistic abundance. The dominant strain, however, at the end of the century is the extreme of illusionism, known best in the work of William Michael Harnett. Harnett's *trompe l'oeil* approach to still life was imitated and practiced by a whole host of other painters, particularly after his return from Europe in 1886. Some of these men, such as John Frederick Peto, John Haberle, and Jefferson Chalfant are today quite well known; one, Martin J. Lawler, is so obscure that the dates of his birth and death are so far unknown. He painted in the area of Erie, Pennsylvania, and his few known still lifes well illustrate the aesthetic change in the approach to that theme at the end of the century. A work of 1879 is a traditional, table-top fruit picture,

Illusionistic
still-life painting

solidly formed, and traditionally illusionistic. Here, the *Trompe l'Oeil Still Life* (cat. no. 25), done ten years later, is a "hanging" still life à la Harnett, where the mixture of objects — the traditional hanging grapes, a torn envelope and letter inscribed with the artist's name, and a newspaper clipping with one edge folded forward — appear to be attached to a wooden board. The eye is barred from penetrating the surface, and as the board-background appears to be the picture plane itself, the objects hanging upon it seem thrust out into the spectator's space. This illusion is enhanced by the sharply realistic technique: the introduction of cast shadows and the penetration of our space by the folded forms — the newspaper clipping and the grape leaf. Further elements of reality are the nails jutting out and the naturalistic appearance of the wood, complete with graining and knots. The picture, incidentally, is painted on canvas board, not on a wooden panel.

Artists such as John Rollin Tilton were extremely well known in their own time and are totally forgotten today. Martin Lawler was obscure in the late 19th century and has remained so. Probably the most mysterious artist in this exhibition is S. S. David, for he does not seem to have existed at all! De Scott Evans, for which S. S. David appears to be a pseudonym (along with Scott David), however, would fall into the first category. He was a Middle Western painter who studied under the academician, Adolphe Bouguereau, in Paris, and worked in Cleveland and New York City. Many of his works were depictions of fashionable women in interiors and out of doors; the paintings were academically constructed though affected by the new concern with light and air. After moving to New York in 1887 he appears to have also become interested in still-life painting. A good number of these combine the luscious realism of mid-century fruit painting with the *trompe l'oeil,* vertical, hanging still life of Harnett; they are paintings of one or more apple or pear against a knotted, grained backdrop. These he sometimes signed with his real name, sometimes "Scott David," and it may be that these works, which in their own time appeared less significant than his ambitious figure pieces, were more and more signed with his alias, allowing the painter to have two artistic personalities, distinct in style, signature and import.

Like the fruit still life, but even more unusual are his many peanut pictures; these, in turn, have the third signature, S. S. David, almost but not quite identical with the pseudonym (the naval connotation of that signature had a tragic, ironic denouement, for the artist lost his life in the 1898 sinking of the "S. S. Bourgogne" on his way to Paris). Here, *Peanuts* (cat. no. 14), is also treated in an extremely *trompe l'oeil* manner; the nuts are seen within a shallow, vertical, glass-fronted case, and the illusionism is increased by the overlapping of projecting nails, broken glass, the card reading "Free Sample Take One" in front of the case itself, and the projection, too, of several of the peanuts from within the case, almost struggling to emerge from the picture space through the broken glass.

What is particularly inexplicable is the popularity of peanut pictures at the time. A whole host of *trompe l'oeil* painters of the period depicted this theme — John Frederick Peto, Joseph Decker, John Haberle, and others. But De Scott Evans's, or S. S. David's, peanut pictures must have attracted many buyers, for no less than five examples are known today; and presumably, even more were painted. All five are extremely similar but not identical: the break in the glass, the position of the card, and the arrangement of the peanuts differ among them. S. S. David's peanut pictures found their imitators, as a rather crude but fascinating example by one S. A. Beers attests.

The history of American painting, particularly during the period of the 19th century, is filled with names which today are unfamiliar to even the most devoted scholars in the field. Many artists who regularly exhibited in the important exhibitions of the time are totally unknown today. Others are known by only one, two, or, at most, a few works, some of which are extremely powerful and extremely beautiful. Perhaps their total production or the general level of their art is inferior to those few examples that remain, and perhaps they did not maintain as consistently high a level of quality as the major masters of the period who appear in the general histories of American art. But surely there are many fine painters and sculptors whose works deserve to be unearthed and studied; indeed, the disappearance of all but a handful of the paintings of many of the artists here exhibited is certainly mysterious. We have tried in this survey to describe the course of American art in the 19th century, not in terms of the famous, but rather, of the obscure and the unknown, believing that this is possible without any sacrifice of quality; the limitations of effecting this with but forty-odd works are obvious. It should be apparent that there is a relative arbitrariness in the selection; certainly one could put forth another forty American painters and sculptors of the period equally obscure and of equal merit. Each and every specialist in the field has favorites among such nearly anonymous masters of earlier years; in the words of De Scott Evans, or Scott David, or S. S. David: "Free Sample, Take One."

Illustrations
Biographies
Check List

JOHN WHITE ALEXANDER (1856-1915)

Born in Allegheny, Pennsylvania, John White Alexander left school
to work as a messenger in a telegraph office there. In the mid-'70s, he
went to New York to study art and work as an illustrator for *Harper's*
where he remained for nearly three years while Thomas Nast, Edwin A.
Abbey, Arthur B. Frost, and Charles Stanley Reinhart were also employed
by the magazine. In the summer of 1877, Alexander sailed for Europe,
settling in Munich after he found it impossible to study in Paris. He
studied at the Munich Academy under Julius Benzcur, but after three
months he joined Frank Duveneck's art class at Polling. Alexander
followed Duveneck to Italy, where he associated with James Abbott
McNeill Whistler, who had a tremendous impact on his work. Returning
to America in 1881, he continued to produce illustrations and established
his reputation as a portrait and figure painter. He traveled in Spain and
Morocco during the '80s but became a Parisian expatriate during the
1890s. He resided in America from the turn of the century, serving as
president of The National Academy of Design from 1909 until his death
in 1915.

1.
Isabella and the Pot of Basil
1897, oil on canvas
75 1/2 x 35 3/4"

Museum of Fine Arts
Boston, Massachusetts
Gift of Ernest Wadsworth Longfellow

2.
French Cottage
1883, oil on canvas
18 x 24"

Newark Museum
Newark, New Jersey

ABRAHAM ARCHIBALD ANDERSON (1847-1940)

Born in New Jersey, Abraham Archibald Anderson was, during his lifetime, recognized first as a painter of Oriental genre scenes, such as *A Street in Cairo* (1875) and *The Young Oriental* (1876), and then as a painter of portraits, such as those of Elihu Root, John Wanamaker, and Oliver Otis Howard. Anderson, like many American painters who reached their maturity in the decade following the Civil War, studied in Paris during the 1880s. After his tutelage with Léon Bonnat, he painted in the studios of Raphael Collin and Fernand Cormon. For the remaining years of the century he divided his time between New York and Paris, where he maintained a studio until 1925. He exhibited frequently in the Paris Salons and was the founder and first president of the American Art Association, which sought to assist American art students in Paris through its library, club room, and exhibitions.

In his late years Anderson maintained an exotic New York studio, which contained, among other treasures, several suits of armor, a 16th-century Venetian doorway, and an elaborate organ. He continued to paint until a week before his death. His long and varied career was not, however, limited to painting; he is also remembered as a rancher, big game hunter. philanthropist, and patron of aviation.

FORTUNATO ARRIOLA (1827-1872)

The self-taught portrait painter and landscapist, Fortunato Arriola, arrived in San Francisco in 1857. He was born and raised in the state of Sinaloa, Mexico, where he studied the classics. The father of a large family, Arriola sought sitters and composed fanciful tropical landscapes from memory in an attempt to support them. In 1871, he went to New York to advance his career and exhibited at the National Academy of Design the following year. He died at sea in 1872, when his ship, bound for California, caught fire in the Atlantic. His fellow San Francisco artists arranged a sale of their own paintings for the benefit of Arriola's family, but the sale only raised a thousand dollars and was considered a failure.

3.
California Landscape
n.d., oil on canvas
30 x 40"

Collection Mr. Morton Bradley
Arlington, Massachusetts

JAMES H. BEARD   (1812-1893)

In the late 1860s, after a successful career as a portrait and genre painter, James H. Beard followed the way of the English engraver Landseer by painting animal allegories such as *The Parson's Pets, Out All Night,* and *A Peep at Growing Danger,* genre scenes featuring domestic animals in the place of people. Like his younger brother, William Holbrook Beard, he used animals "to suggest a moral, or, perhaps, a satire on the frailties or vanities of human life."

Born in Buffalo, New York, Beard moved with his family to Painesville, Ohio, in 1823. By the age of seventeen he had taken lessons from an itinerant portrait painter and launched an artistic career that would take him throughout the Middle West and South to such cities as Pittsburgh, Cincinnati, Louisville, and New Orleans. He eventually painted the portraits of such notable figures as Henry Clay, General William Henry Harrison, and General Zachary Taylor. He also produced a number of frontier genre scenes such as *The Long Bill, The Land Speculator,* and *The North Carolina Emigrants;* these scenes are reminiscent of the work of his contemporary George Caleb Bingham in subject and composition. Beard settled in Cincinnati in 1834, and with the exception of a brief sojourn in New York in 1846-47 and his period of service in the Civil War, he made this Ohio city his home until 1870. After that year, he worked in Flushing, Long Island, and in New York City, where he became a member of the National Academy in 1872.

James H. Beard was the oldest member of the talented Beard family. His brother, sons, and nephew all made significant contributions to American painting, illustration, and literature.

4.
The Parson's Pets
1874, oil on canvas
27 x 22"

Anonymous

WILLIAM HOLBROOK BEARD   (1824-1900)

The younger brother and student of James H. Beard, William Holbrook Beard made his reputation with humorous and satirical paintings of animals engaged in human activities. His pictures of bears and monkeys, such as *The Bears of Wall Street Celebrating a Drop in the Market* (New-York Historical Society), are perhaps his best-known works, although he occasionally attempted more serious subjects such as *The Star of Bethlehem* and *The End of Time.*

Born in Painesville, Ohio, he began his career by painting portraits; later, during the early 1850s, he maintained a studio in Buffalo, New York. Between 1856 and 1858, Beard toured Europe, visiting Düsseldorf, Paris, and Rome. He returned to Buffalo in 1858 and married the daughter of the genre painter Thomas Le Clear. Settling in New York in 1861, he opened a studio in the Tenth Street Building after 1866. Although Beard is remembered as a painter, he also designed at least two sculptural monuments, neither of which was executed: a colossal figure, representing California, for James Lick, and around 1870, a plan for subterranean entrances to an art gallery proposed for Central Park for the millionaire, Henry Keep.

Beard died in 1900, after lamenting the state of American art in the 1890s and calling for a return to a national art that was "unpretentious, earnest and direct."

5.
Susannah and the Elders
1865, oil on canvas
15 1/4 x 21"

Collection Mr. Henry M. Fuller
New York, New York

6.
The Italian Bead Stringers
1887/1888, oil on canvas
30 1/4 x 40 3/4"

The Otesaga Hotel
Cooperstown, New York

ROBERT FREDERICK BLUM (1857-1903)

Illustrator, printmaker, and painter of pastels, as well as an easel and mural painter, Robert Frederick Blum worked as a lithographer and illustrator for *Scribner's*. Born in Cincinnati, Ohio, he received his limited artistic training there, where he was friendly with John Henry Twachtman and Kenyon Cox, and in Philadelphia, where his painting style was affected by seeing the work of the Europeans Mariano J. M. B. Fortuny and Giovanni Boldini at the Centennial Exposition in 1876. In 1880, he left for Europe, meeting Frank Duveneck and James Abbott McNeill Whistler in Venice; there he developed his etching and pastel techniques. Under Whistler's influence, his paintings show a change from draftsmanlike realism to a greater emphasis on the immediate impression created by light and atmosphere. During the early '80s, he visited Spain and Holland, often in the company of William Merritt Chase. Upon his return to New York in 1885, he occupied J. Alden Weir's old studio and there completed his first important oil painting, *Venetian Lace Makers.* Having been commissioned by *Scribner's* to illustrate Sir Edwin Arnold's book *Japonica,* Blum left for a two-year sojourn in Japan in 1890, becoming one of the first American artists to travel there. While in Japan, he sent back many illustrations to *Scribner's* and painted *The Ameya,* for which he was elected to the National Academy in 1892. The next year he began work on his murals for the Mendelssohn Glee Club in New York. At the time of his death in 1903, he was at work on a mural for the New Amsterdam Theater in New York.

ALFRED BOISSEAU (1823-1901)

Born in Paris, the portrait and genre painter Alfred Boisseau is one
of the many European artists, including Jean Joseph Vaudechamp, the
French painter, and Dominique Canova, the Italian sculptor, who visited
New Orleans in the middle of the 19th century. Before his arrival there
in 1845, Boisseau had exhibited at the Salon in Paris. Between 1849 and
1852 he was living in New York, exhibiting at The National Academy of
Design and the American Art-Union during that time. By late 1852, he
had settled in Cleveland, Ohio, where he advertised his talents as a portrait
and landscape painter and as an art teacher and dealer. He is known to
have been in Cleveland as late as 1859; after that date, he settled in
Montreal, where he painted society portraits. Boisseau died in Buffalo,
New York, in 1901.

7.
(Marche d'Indiens) Louisiana
Indians Walking Along the Bayou
1847, oil on canvas
24 x 40"

New Orleans Museum of Art
New Orleans, Louisiana

8.
Still Life
1862, oil on canvas
34 x 44"

E. B. Crocker Art Gallery
Sacramento, California

SAMUEL MARSDEN BROOKES (1816-1892)

Born in Middlesex, England, Samuel Marsden Brookes, immigrated
with his parents to Chicago in 1832. He moved to Milwaukee, Wisconsin,
in 1842, the year after he had begun painting, and remained there until
1862, except for a winter he spent studying in England in 1845-46. During the next decade he painted portraits, miniatures, and landscapes, and
between 1855 and 1858, worked in partnership with Thomas H.
Stevenson.

It was not until 1858 that Brookes painted his first still life, a game
piece, which, along with hanging fruit, became typical of his *oeuvre* for
the next three decades. Brookes's artistic significance lies in his accom-
plished treatment of the relatively unusual game theme and in his role in
the development of American art in San Francisco. He had settled there
in 1862, joining an active group of artists that included Edwin Deakin and
William Keith. Soon after his arrival, he helped to establish the San
Francisco Artists' Union, a forerunner of the San Francisco Art Association, of which he was the first vice-president in 1871. During the early
1870s he was also an active member of the Bohemian Club. Besides his
still lifes of trophies of the hunt and stream, Brookes also painted live
animals — the squirrel, the dog, and his much-praised *Peacock* (1880).

GEORGE LORING BROWN   (1814-1889)

Often called the "American Claude," George Loring Brown began his career as a wood engraver in Boston, where he was born in 1814. His success as an artist, however, was achieved as a painter of the Italian *campagna,* and later, the New England landscape. During his student days in Paris in the 1830s, he financed his training in the studio of Eugène Isabey by making copies of the Old Masters in the Louvre. Washington Allston, an early supporter of Brown's career, pronounced his *The Meeting of Mark Anthony and Cleopatra* "the best copy of Claude Lorraine (*sic*) he had ever seen."

After 1840, Brown made his residence in Italy, dividing his time between Florence and Rome for the next twenty years. Nathaniel Hawthorne described him in the *Marble Faun* as "an artist who has studied Nature with such tender love that she takes him to her intimacy, enabling him to reproduce her in landscapes that seem the reality of a better earth." Upon his return to the United States in 1859, Brown lived briefly in New York, but after 1864, worked in Boston. He is reported to have painted sixty important landscapes and innumerable copies of the Old Masters, as well as portraits and miniatures, during a career that spanned more than five decades.

9.
Tivoli
1850, oil on canvas
24 1/2 x 31 1/2"

Newark Museum
Newark, New Jersey

WILLIAM MASON BROWN   (1828-1898)

Born in Troy, New York, William Mason Brown lived for a brief time in Newark, New Jersey, then settled in Brooklyn by 1859, remaining there until his death.

Brown began his career as a landscapist in the romantic tradition established by Thomas Cole. In the 1860s, after a dozen years of painting in this style, he abruptly switched his technique and subject matter, producing still lifes rendered with almost photographic realism. Many of his fruit pieces were reproduced in lithograph, earning him widespread recognition as a creator of still life.

After his arrival in New York, in 1859, Brown exhibited regularly at the National Academy of Design until 1890.

10.
Raspberries
n.d., oil on canvas
20 x 16"

The J. B. Speed Art Museum
Louisville, Kentucky

GEORGE DE FOREST BRUSH (1855-1941)

The portrait painter George de Forest Brush returned to two themes throughout his career: the Madonna and Child and the Indian. His Indian pictures resulted from the four years he spent traveling and sketching in the northern plains region of the United States and in Canada, but rather than realistically depicting Indian life, costumes, and customs, his interpretations are romantic. As a contemporary critic commented, "his work is like opening a window and looking out into another age, upon another race, almost in another world."

Born in Shelbyville, Tennessee, Brush was raised in Connecticut. He was in Paris between 1874 and 1880, studying with Gérôme. During his student years he visited Florence and later painted there for part of each year until the outbreak of World War I.

In 1888, Brush won the National Academy of Design's Hallgarten Prize and was elected an associate of the Academy that same year. Shortly thereafter, he opened his studio in Dublin, New Hampshire, which became his residence until it was destroyed by fire in 1937 — along with many of his paintings. He continued to paint until his death in 1941.

11.
Mother and Child
1895, oil on panel
38 1/2 x 38 1/2" (tondo)

Museum of Fine Arts
Boston, Massachusetts
William Wilkins Warren Fund

12.
The Pool, Medfield
1889, oil on canvas
18 x 24"

Museum of Fine Arts
Boston, Massachusetts
Emily L. Ainsley Fund

DENNIS MILLER BUNKER   (1861-1890)

The brief artistic career of Dennis Miller Bunker began with his study at The National Academy of Design and the Art Students League under William Merritt Chase. He also studied landscape painting with Charles Melville Dewey. In 1882, Bunker left for France, where he spent a few months at the Académie Julian under Hébert, later entering the atelier of Gérôme at the École des Beaux-Arts.

Returning to America in 1884 or 1885, Bunker settled in Boston for the next four years and is usually associated with that city, probably because he taught at the Cowles School there and met Isabella Stewart Gardner, his enthusiastic patron. During this period, he painted his sensitive portrait of *Miss Anne Page* (1887) and several still lifes which he presented to his friends as gifts. His early landscapes, with their overall tonalism, are allied to American Barbizon painting. It was not until his association with John Singer Sargent at Calcott, England, in the summer of 1888 that Bunker's work began to show a truly Impressionist concern for the colorful effects of light and atmosphere. Back in America the following year, he painted some of his finest Impressionist landscapes at Medfield, Massachusetts.

To quote Royal Cortissoz, "he was untimely lost," dying in 1890, shortly after his marriage and move to New York.

GEORGE COMEGYS (c. 1816-after 1852)

The genre, portrait, and historical painter George Comegys was born in Maryland and died in Philadelphia; little else is known about him. *The Little Plunderers, The Ghost Story,* and *Boys Stealing Watermelons* are characteristic of his painterly technique and his choice of subject matter, where humor is achieved through exaggerated facial expression and distorted anatomy.

Comegys studied with the Philadelphia portraitist John Neagle in the 1830s, his earliest extant work being a copy of Neagle's *Pat Lyon at the Forge* (1836). Comegys exhibited at The Pennsylvania Academy, The National Academy of Design, the Apollo Association, and the Artists' Fund Society, of which in 1845 he was a member of the board.

13.
Boys Stealing Watermelons
1839, oil on canvas
16 7/8 x 19 3/4"

Collection Mr. James H. Ricau
Piermont, New York

S. S. DAVID (1847-1898)

The artist "S. S. David" was born De Scott Evans in Boston, Indiana. Primarily a portrait and genre painter, he taught in the Middle West before going to Paris to study with Adolphe Bouguereau in 1877. The following year he returned to Cleveland, where he remained for almost a decade as teacher and co-director of the Cleveland Academy of Fine Arts before leaving for New York in 1887. He appears to have painted his still lifes after this date.

De Scott Evans altered his signature several times: early in his career he signed his work "D. S. Evans" or "D. Scott Evans"; he signed his still lifes of hanging fruit "Scott David," a reversal of his first two names; finally, he signed "S. S. David" to a group of still lifes which depict peanuts within a glass-fronted case. He lost his life in a naval disaster in 1898 while en route to Paris to execute a ceiling painting.

14.
Peanuts
n.d., oil on canvas
11 7/8 x 10"

Portland Art Museum
Portland, Oregon

SARAH PAXTON BALL DODSON (1847-1909)

Born in Philadelphia, Sarah Paxton Ball Dodson was the daughter of Richard Whatcoat Dodson, an engraver, illustrator, and portraitist. By 1872 she had begun studying at The Pennsylvania Academy of the Fine Arts under Christian Schussele. Later she continued her training in Paris with Evariste Vital Luminais and Jules Lefebvre. Her early work reflects these academic influences, but in her mature style she developed what John E. D. Trask has described as "poetic idealism." Sarah Dodson frequently exhibited at the Paris Salon, beginning in 1879, and spent her later years in Brighton, England. The artist was always in delicate health, particularly after a serious illness in 1893, but she worked until her death in January, 1909.

15.
The Bacidae
1883, oil on canvas
79 1/4 x 61 11/16"

Indianapolis Museum of Art
Indianapolis, Indiana
Gift of Richard B. Dodson

16.
Cheyenne Camp
1892, watercolor on paper
12 x 24"

Cincinnati Art Museum
Cincinnati, Ohio
Gift of William Procter in
memory of Harley T. Procter

HENRY F. FARNY (1847-1916)

The artist Henry F. Farny was a magazine and newspaper illustrator for most of his career, but after 1890, he devoted much of his artistic energy to painting the life of the American Indian.

Farny was born in Ribeauville in the French province of Alsace in 1847, but his father, a Republican, brought the family to the United States when Napoleon III established the second Empire. The Farny family settled in Warren, Pennsylvania, in 1853 and six years later moved to Cincinnati, which remained Farny's permanent residence, despite trips to Europe and to the American West. In the late 1860s, he worked for a short time in New York as an illustrator for *Harper's* and then set sail for a three-year stay in Europe, where he was befriended by the American T. Buchanan Read in Rome and by the Hungarian Munkácsy in Düsseldorf. After a brief return to Cincinnati in 1870 to sell his pictures, Farny went back to Europe, this time to Vienna and Munich, where he studied with Wilhelm Diez and spent some time with his fellow Cincinnati artist, Frank Duveneck. Upon returning home, Farny made many sketching trips in the West: in 1881, he went to the Sioux agency at Standing Rock; in 1883, he traveled with the Henry Villard excursion, which witnessed the completion of the transcontinental railroad; in 1884, he visited Montana again with Eugene Smalley to produce an article for *Century Magazine;* and it is believed that he made additional trips later in the decade.

MANUEL JOACHIM DE FRANCA   (1808-1865)

Born either in Funchal, Madeira, or Oporto, Portugal, Manuel Joachim de Franca arrived in Philadelphia around 1830, remaining there until 1842; he exhibited at the Pennsylvania Academy of the Fine Arts, the Artists' Fund Society, Apollo Association, and The National Academy of Design. By 1847, he had settled in St. Louis, Missouri, where he stayed until his death in 1865. He is known for his portraits, especially for that of Henry Clay, as well as his historical and religious pictures. His work was sometimes engraved.

17.
Portrait of Matthew Hinzinga Messchert
1839, oil on canvas
50 1/8 x 40 1/4"

Philadelphia Museum of Art
Philadelphia, Pennsylvania
Gift of Dr. and Mrs. Harold Lefft

WALTER GAY (1856-1937)

An expatriate who studied and lived in France for more than sixty years, Walter Gay associated with such Americans there as Henry James, James Abbott McNeill Whistler, Mary Cassatt, and John Singer Sargent. Born in Hingham, Massachusetts, in 1856, he was the nephew of the landscapist, Winckworth Allan Gay. He began his artistic career as a flower painter in Boston and turned to figure painting after studying in Paris with Léon Bonnat for three years, beginning in 1876. At his teacher's suggestion, he made a trip to Spain in 1878 to see work by Jusepe de Ribera and Diego Velázquez; the following year he successfully exhibited *The Fencing Lesson* and a landscape at the Paris Salon. By 1895, however, he had restricted the range of his subject matter to paintings of interiors, usually those of the French 18th century. Gay became an authority on 18th-century drawings and decorative objects. After his death in 1937, his widow gave his collection of paintings and drawings, including works by Nicolas Lancret, François Boucher, and Jean-Honoré Fragonard, to the Louvre.

18.
Wild Flowers
1875, oil on canvas
25 x 19"

Yale University Art Gallery
New Haven, Connecticut
John Hill Morgan, B. A. 1893,
Fund, 1972.62

SAMUEL LANCASTER GERRY (1813-1891)

    The self-taught artist Samuel Lancaster Gerry passed most of his life in Boston, where he was born in 1813, and in the New England countryside, particularly in the White Mountains of New Hampshire. Although he painted portraits as well as genre and animal scenes, he is remembered for his landscapes. Around 1849, Gerry made a three-year trip to Europe, chiefly to Rome and Florence, where he associated with the sculptors Horatio Greenough and Hiram Powers and the painters William Page and John G. Chapman. Upon his return, Gerry became one of the leading exponents of the "White Mountain school," devoting his career to a subject which had attracted such Hudson River landscapists as Thomas Cole and Asher B. Durand. In his later years he turned to journalism, writing articles on art for the *New England Magazine.*

19.
Sunset
n.d., oil on canvas
29 1/4 x 24 1/4"

Collection Mr. Morton Bradley
Arlington, Massachusetts

20.
Summer at Campobello, New Brunswick
ca. 1890-1900, oil on canvas
28 x 28"

Museum of Fine Arts
Boston, Massachusetts
Bequest of Maxim Karolik

EDWARD WILBUR DEAN HAMILTON   (1864-1934)

The portrait and landscape painter Edward Wilbur Dean Hamilton was born in Somerfield, Pennsylvania, but spent most of his artistic career in the Boston area. He studied at the École des Beaux-Arts in Paris, where he was exposed to Impressionist painting, and in the late 1880s traveled to Italy, where he captured Venetian light and atmosphere in his canvases. Settling in Boston upon his return, he became a member of the Boston Guild of Artists and taught at the Massachusetts School of Art, Boston University, and the Rhode Island School of Design. During the 1890s, he exhibited at the Society of American Artists in New York, but continued to list his address as Boston, where he died in 1934.

JAMES HAMILTON (1819-1878)

Born in Antrim, near Belfast, Ireland, James Hamilton came to Philadelphia with his parents at the age of fifteen. After receiving encouragement from John Sartain, he established himself in Philadelphia as a landscapist and a teacher of drawing. He began exhibiting at the Artists' Fund Society in 1840 and subsequently showed his work in Washington, Baltimore, New York, and Boston, as well as in Philadelphia. He made a trip to London in 1854-55. Hamilton died in San Francisco in 1878 on the first leg of a trip around the world.

The contemporary writer, Henry Tuckerman described James Hamilton's style as "bold and free; he does not aim at high finish; he is the reverse of the literal, and aims to give emphatically his own feeling and sense of a subject." Hamilton's marine paintings, such as *Foundering* and *Old Ironsides,* are executed with a painterly brushstroke and an imaginative flair that have earned him the title of the "American Turner." His most famous painting is *The Last Days of Pompeii.* During his own lifetime, however, he was probably equally well known for his illustrations of Dr. Elisha Kent Kane's *The U. S. Grinnell Expedition in Search of Sir John Franklin* (1854) and *Arctic Explorations...* (1857).

21.
Old Ironsides
1863, oil on canvas
60 1/2 x 48"

Pennsylvania Academy of the Fine Arts
Philadelphia, Pennsylvania
Gift of Caroline Gibson Taitt, 1885

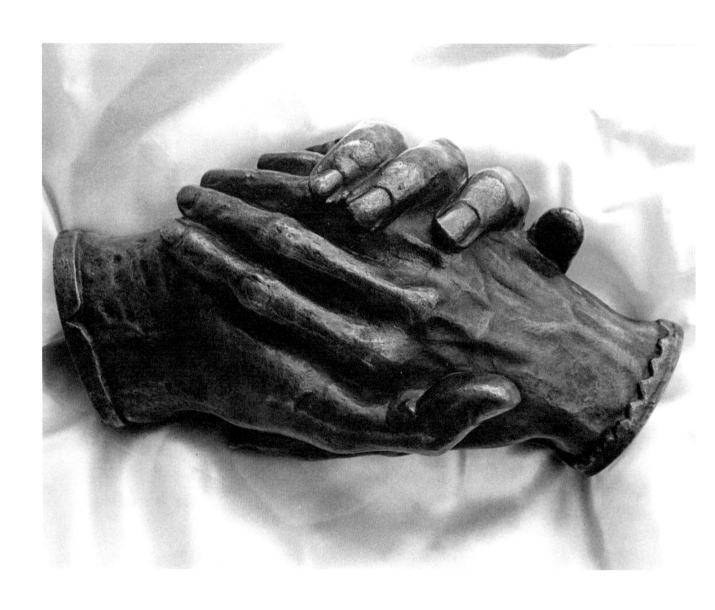

22.
Hands of Robert and Elizabeth Browning
1853, cast bronze
3 1/4 x 4 1/2 x 8 1/4"

Armstrong Browning Library
Waco, Texas

HARRIET HOSMER (1830-1908)

Perhaps the most prominent member of the group of American women sculptors living in Europe in mid-century, Harriet Hosmer astounded her Victorian generation with athletic and artistic accomplishments. Undaunted by social strictures, she pursued the career of a sculptor, causing Henry Tuckerman to comment that "her most obvious characteristic from childhood was strength of purpose." Born in Watertown, Massachusetts, in 1830, she began her career in the late 1840s, taking lessons from the Boston sculptor Paul Stevenson. These lessons were followed in 1850 by the study of anatomy at a medical school in Columbia, Missouri. At this time, she traveled in the Middle West and made a trip down the Mississippi on a riverboat. In 1852, after she completed her first sculpture, a bust variously called *Hesper* or *Evening Star,* her friend, the actress Charlotte Cushman, encouraged her to go to Italy to study. There she worked for seven years with John Gibson, the most prominent English neoclassicist in Rome. During this Roman period, she executed some of her most important sculptures, including the *Beatrice Cenci, Puck,* and *Hands of Robert and Elizabeth Browning* (opposite). In 1860, she visited her friends and family in America, and in 1862, she exhibited her monumental *Zenobia* at the Crystal Palace in London. Harriet Hosmer lived in England until the end of the century, but died in America in 1908, eight years after her return from Europe.

DAVID JOHNSON (1827-1908)

At his death just after the turn of the century, David Johnson was described as "one of the strongest and best known of American landscape painters of the middle of the last century." He studied briefly with Jasper F. Cropsey and began his career as a Hudson River landscapist and "close student of nature." He was born in New York in 1827 and spent most of his time there, never traveling abroad; rather, he went on sketching trips to New England and upstate New York. By the 1870s, however, he was painting in the Barbizon style and was referred to as the "American Rousseau." He was elected to The National Academy of Design in 1861, and in 1876 received a medal at the Philadelphia Centennial Exhibition. When he exhibited *Housatonic River* at the Paris Salon the following year, it too was well received. In spite of his successful career, from which he is reported to have amassed a fortune, Johnson never married and remained somewhat of a recluse.

23.
Old Mill, West Milford, New Jersey
1850, oil on canvas
16 1/8 x 22 1/4"

The Brooklyn Museum
Brooklyn, New York

GEORGE COCHRAN LAMBDIN (1830-1896)

Born in Pittsburgh, Pennsylvania, George Cochran Lambdin spent
most of his artistic career in Philadelphia, where he studied with his father,
James Reid Lambdin, and exhibited at The Pennsylvania Academy of the
Fine Arts after 1848. He visited Europe in 1855 and 1870, and resided in
New York for two years beginning in 1868, at which time he was elected
to The National Academy of Design.

Lambdin established his reputation as a painter of sentimental genre
pictures which often featured children and of Civil War scenes which depicted soldiers in camp or at home rather than in battle. In the late 1860s,
he turned to still life, becoming one of Philadelphia's leading still-life
artists and, certainly, the best-known flower painter at that time. He
painted bouquet pictures, usually of roses but sometimes including many
different types of flowers arranged together. After 1870, when he settled
in Germantown, outside of Philadelphia, and cultivated a flower garden,
Lambdin began to paint roses as they actually grew in his garden. These
still lifes show a new interest in the natural setting and in the effects of
light and atmosphere. At the same time, he also adopted a flat, shiny
background for other paintings of growing roses, originating a still-life
format which became the vogue during the 1870s.

24.
Roses
1874, oil on canvas
20 x 16"

Collection Mr. and Mrs. William C. Burt
Upper Montclair, New Jersey

MARTIN J. LAWLER (unknown)

A painter of fruit pieces during the 1870s, Martin J. Lawler a decade later, turned to illusionistic works depicting hanging fruit or game against a flat board background. He appears to have been active in northwestern Pennsylvania, where he worked in Erie in 1889, perhaps as an itinerant. Local newspapers suggest that he lived in Union City, Pennsylvania, and either Conneaut, Ohio, or Conneautville, Pennsylvania.

25.
Trompe l'Oeil Still Life
n.d., oil on canvas board
16 1/2 x 16 1/2"

Office of State History
Schenectady, New York

26.
Pleasant Valley, Essex
County, New York
1867, oil on canvas
24 x 36"

Yale University Art Gallery
New Haven, Connecticut
Gift of Mrs. Edward F. Dwight,
1955.46.1

ALEXANDER LAWRIE (1828-1917)

Born in New York to a family of Scottish immigrants, Alexander Lawrie is remembered for his landscapes and for his portraits in both oil and crayon. He began his career as an apprentice to a New York wood engraver between 1843 and 1852, and during the final years of his apprenticeship, he studied painting and became a student at The National Academy of Design. When his family moved to Indiana in 1852, Lawrie settled in Philadelphia, where he exhibited at The Pennsylvania Academy of the Fine Arts in 1852 and 1854. In the summer of 1855, he left for Europe, spending most of his two years abroad studying with Emanuel Leutze in Düsseldorf, although he stopped briefly in Paris and Florence. Upon his return in 1857, he continued to work in Philadelphia, and in 1860, he enrolled as a student at the Pennsylvania Academy. In 1861, he enlisted in the infantry, being discharged after two years of service with the kidney ailment which plagued him for the rest of his life.

Throughout the 1860s and '70s, Lawrie spent his winters in New York and his summers in the Adirondacks, the Hudson Highlands, or the Lake George region of New York State, where he became friendly with such American landscapists as Asher B. Durand, Homer Martin, and Jervis McEntee. After this successful period, during which he was elected an associate of the National Academy, Lawrie left New York, traveling to Hartford, Connecticut, parts of Indiana, and to Chicago in search of commissions. He returned to New York between 1890 and 1895, and, in 1896 joined his family in Chalmers, Indiana. In 1902, he was admitted to the State Soldiers Home in Lafayette, Indiana, where he painted a series of about 150 Civil War portraits until his death in 1917.

JERVIS MCENTEE   (1828-1891)

Born in Rondout, New York, Jervis McEntee spent much of his life there, except for those winter months which he passed working in his New York studio. He studied with Frederic Church in the winter of 1850-51, but did not embark on his professional career until 1858, after a rather disasterous business venture. In 1861, he was elected to The National Academy of Design and achieved his first great success with *Melancholy Day,* an autumnal scene based on William Cullen Bryant's poem, "The Death of the Flowers." In 1869 he made his only trip to Europe, with Sanford Robinson Gifford, and while in Italy collaborated with George Healy and his former teacher Frederic Church on *The Arch of Titus* (1871). In his *Book of the Artists,* Henry T. Tuckerman praises McEntee for his ability to portray the seasons, particularly autumn and winter.

27.
A Skating Party
1890, oil on canvas
30 x 36"

Collection Mr. Robert C. Vose, Jr.
Boston, Massachusetts

FREDERICK MACMONNIES (1863-1937)

Typical of our late-19th-century sculptors, Frederick MacMonnies, who was born in Brooklyn, was trained in the French Beaux-Arts style in the 1880s in Paris. He was a student of Jean Alexandre Falguière at the École des Beaux-Arts, after spending four years as a studio assistant to Augustus Saint-Gaudens in New York. In Paris, he won the Prix d'Atelier for two consecutive years and exhibited at the Salons. A Parisian cholera epidemic sent MacMonnies to Munich, where he studied painting rather than sculpture. By 1901, he had achieved "a second reputation not inferior to that which he already enjoyed" in sculpture after he exhibited paintings at the Salon anonymously and won honors. It is as a sculptor, however, that MacMonnies is remembered today, particularly for his *Bacchante with Infant Faun* (1893) and his *Triumph of Columbia* which appeared at the World's Columbian Exposition, Chicago, that same year. Between 1905 and 1913, he maintained a studio-school at Giverny outside of Paris, where he was surrounded by a group of admiring young sculptors, including his student, Janet Scudder, and where he executed his statues of General Slocum for New York City and General McClellan for Washington, D. C. During the 1940s, he worked on allegorical pieces, including the *Civic Virtue.* MacMonnies died of pneumonia in New York in 1937.

28.
Portrait of the Artist
n.d., oil on canvas
37 13/16 x 32 1/16"

The Metropolitan Museum of Art
New York, New York
Purchase, Mrs. James Fosburgh Gift,
1967

LOUIS REMY MIGNOT   (1831-1870)

Born in Charleston, South Carolina, Louis Remy Mignot studied drawing there before leaving for Holland at the age of 20 to continue his artistic training. By 1855, he had returned to America, and settled in New York, remaining there until the outbreak of the Civil War.

In 1857, Mignot made an important trip to Ecuador with his fellow landscape painter Frederic Church; the landscapes which Mignot painted as a result of this trip prompted Henry T. Tuckerman to describe him as one "whose nativity, temperament, and taste combined to make him the efficient delineator of tropical atmosphere and vegetation." In 1858, he was elected to the National Academy and collaborated with Thomas P. Rossiter on *Washington and Lafayette at Mount Vernon* (1859; The Metropolitan Museum of Art).

In 1862, loyal to his southern sympathies, Mignot left the city where his work had found enthusiastic support and made his residence in Brighton, England, until his death in 1870.

29.
On the Guayaquil
n.d., oil on canvas
17 x 25 1/8"

Collection Mr. and Mrs. Will Richeson, Jr.
San Marino, California

30.
Sculptor's Studio
n.d., oil on canvas
29 1/16 x 36 1/4"

The Metropolitan Museum of Art
New York, New York
Purchase, The Bertram F. and Susie
Brummer Foundation, Inc., Gift, 1967

LOUIS MOELLER (1855-1930)

Born in New York in 1855, Moeller studied at The National
Academy of Design where he won the Academy's Hallgarten Prize in 1884
for his small painting, *Puzzled.* He was elected a member of the Academy
a little over a decade later.

He also studied in Munich for six years with Wilhelm Diez and the
American, Frank Duveneck, absorbing their interest in figures in interior
scenes, painted with a dark, limited palette. He occasionally essayed more
lavish genre scenes, such as *The Antique Shop* (ca. 1895), which depicts
many figures in an interior that is crowded with the bric-a-brac cherished
by the late 19th century. Moeller maintained a studio in the Paramount
Building in New York, but made his residence in Weehawken, New Jersey.
By the time of his death in 1930, he had long been too ill to paint and
was nearly forgotten.

SAMUEL MURRAY (1870-1941)

Unlike many artists of his generation, the sculptor Samuel Murray who was born in Philadelphia, never went abroad to work or study; his only teacher was Thomas Eakins, with whom he studied at the Art Students League of Philadelphia in 1887. Murray executed two portraits of his former teacher – *Thomas Eakins* (1894) and *Thomas Eakins Cross-Legged with His Palette* (1907). A close friendship developed between the two men, and they collaborated on the sculptural project on the Witherspoon Building in Philadelphia in 1895-96.

In 1891, Eakins secured a position for Murray as sculpture instructor at the Moore Institute, formerly the Philadelphia School for Design, where he taught for nearly fifty years. Among his better-known works are his statues of Commodore Bardry in Independence Square, Philadelphia, and Senator Boies Penrose in Harrisburg, Pennsylvania, as well as his Pennsylvania State Memorial in Gettysburg and his Bishop Shanahan Memorial also in Harrisburg.

Murray received honorable mention in the Chicago World's Columbian Exposition (1893) and the Buffalo Exposition (1901); he was awarded a silver medal at the St. Louis Exposition (1904). He died in 1941 at the age of seventy-one after a long illness.

31.
Boxer
1899, bronze
30 1/2 x 22 x 10"

Yale University Art Gallery
New Haven, Connecticut
Whitney Collections of Sporting Art,
given in memory of Harry Payne
Whitney, B. A. 1894, and Payne
Whitney, B. A. 1898, by Francis P.
Garvin, B. A. 1897, 1932.202

32.
A Painter's Dream
1869, oil on canvas
29 3/4 x 28 1/2"

The Detroit Institute of Arts
Detroit, Michigan
Gift of Charles E. Feinberg in honor
of Mrs. Benjamin L. Lambert's 90th
Birthday

THOMAS BUCHANAN READ (1822-1872)

Born in 1822, Thomas Buchanan Read ran away from his Chester County, Pennsylvania, home in 1835, after being apprenticed to a tailor, and two years later settled in Cincinnati, where he was an assistant to the sculptor, Shobal V. Clevenger. Read became friendly with a group of sculptors who had gathered around Henry Kirke Brown, and began his career as a portrait painter. By 1841, his portrait commissions had declined and he moved to Boston, where his efforts as an artist were encouraged by Washington Allston and his talents as a poet were recognized by Henry Wadsworth Longfellow. He painted portraits and wrote poetry in Philadelphia between 1846 and 1850, at which time he departed for Europe. Read stopped in England, making the acquaintance of the Pre-Raphaelites, and in Düsseldorf, visiting Emanuel Leutze, but his primary interest was in Italy, where he would spend the final two decades of his life, except for occasional visits to the United States.

During the Civil War, he returned to work for the Union cause, serving on the staff of Lew Wallace as a lecturer and propagandist. It was at this time that he wrote his patriotic poem "Sheridan's Ride," a theme he later depicted on canvas. Tuckerman praises both his painting and his poetry for "a certain grace of conception and refinement of execution" but admits that Read "is, perhaps, better known by his verses than his pictures." In 1872, he returned to America and died a week after his arrival in New York.

ROBERT REID (1862-1929)

Born in Stockbridge, Massachusetts, Robert Reid studied at the Boston Museum School, the Art Students League of New York, and the Académie Julian in Paris during the 1880s. One of the founding members of "The Ten American Painters," he developed an impressionist technique which he often applied to his favorite subject, the contemplative female figure. Reid also worked as a designer of stained glass and as a mural painter. He helped decorate the Liberal Arts Building of the Chicago World's Columbian Exposition in 1893, and, four years later, completed his murals at the Library of Congress in Washington, D. C. He exhibited extensively, winning medals at the World's Columbian Exposition, The National Academy of Design (1898), the Exposition Universelle (1900), the Pan-American Exposition (1901), the Universal Exposition (1904), and the Panama-Pacific Exposition (1915). Even after suffering a stroke in 1927, he was able to exhibit work executed with his left hand after his right side had been paralyzed. At the time of his death in 1929, he was recognized as an internationally-known artist.

33.
Violet Kimono
n.d., oil on canvas
28 1/2 x 24 3/4"

National Collection of Fine Arts
Washington, D. C.

34.
Such is Life, A Scene in
London During the Crimean War
1855, oil on canvas
19 1/2 x 27 1/2"

Newark Museum
Newark, New Jersey

THOMAS P. ROSSITER (1818-1871)

The historical, religious, and portrait painter Thomas P. Rossiter was born in 1818 in New Haven, Connecticut, where he later began his artistic training under a local portraitist, Nathaniel Jocelyn. In 1838 he exhibited at the National Academy and the following year he moved to New York, opened his own studio and became friendly with John F. Kensett. In 1840, he sailed for Europe with Kensett, James Casilear, and Asher B. Durand; he remained abroad for six years, spending his time primarily in Paris, Florence, Venice, and Rome. His *Studio Reception* (1841), which portrays such artists as Daniel Huntington and George Healy, suggests his friendship with many of the Americans then working in Europe. Among the paintings he produced during this first European trip were *Rebecca at the Well* and *Return of the Dove to the Arc.* Returning to New York, he was elected to the National Academy in 1849 and shared a studio with John Kensett and Louis Lang. In 1853, the artist made a second Grand Tour of Europe, this time with his wife of two years, Anna Parmly Rossiter. After his wife's death in childbirth in 1856, he settled again in New York, where he devoted much of his career to historical and religious painting, including *Washington and Lafayette at Mount Vernon* (1859; The Metropolitan Museum of Art), a collaborative painting with Louis Mignot. He spent the final decade of his career with his second wife Mollie Sterling in Cold Spring, New York, where he worked on a series of paintings depicting *The Life of Christ.*

CHRISTIAN SCHUSSELE [SCHUSSELLE] (1824 or 1826-1879)

Christian Schussele, the genre, portrait, and historical painter, first achieved success as a lithographer. Born in Alsace, he studied lithography with one of the brothers, Jean Baptiste or Gabriel Christophe Guerin, at the Academy of Strasbourg and painting with Paul Delaroche in Paris, where he also designed illustrations for the publishing house of Engelman and Graf. Louis Philippe conceived the idea of having a series of chromolithographs of the pictures at Versailles prepared, and Schussele was given the commission. This scheme was ended abruptly by the revolution of 1848, however. He decided to immigrate to Philadelphia, where he worked as a chromolithographer and wood engraver. He remained relatively unknown until 1851, when he exhibited *The Artists' Recreation* at The Pennsylvania Academy of the Fine Arts and established his reputation as a painter. After 1854, he turned to history painting, several examples of which were engraved by John Sartain. Schussele continued to work at his former occupation, however, traveling throughout the South in the employ of a bank-note company. In 1863, he was stricken with a palsy and departed for Europe to seek a cure for this affliction, which would trouble him for the rest of his life. Upon his return in 1868, he was unanimously elected Professor of Drawing and Painting at the Pennsylvania Academy, a newly created position which he held until his death in 1879.

35.
The Young Recruits (Mock Army)
1855, oil on canvas
39 1/4 x 52 1/2"

Collection Dr. and Mrs. Henry C.
Landon, III
North Wilkesboro, North Carolina

36.
***Buffalo Harbor from
the Foot of Porter Avenue***
1871, oil on canvas
18 x 30"

Albright-Knox Art Gallery
Buffalo, New York
Gift of Henry A. Richmond

LARS SELLSTEDT (1819-1911)

Before he settled permanently in Buffalo, New York, in 1846, Lars Sellstedt had worked as a sailor and rigger, and had received some instruction in painting from a Captain Black. In the late 1840s, he opened a studio in Buffalo, attended lectures at Buffalo Medical School, and became engaged to Linda Lovejoy, who unfortunately died in 1850 in the first year of their marriage. In 1856, he married Caroline Scott, whose socially prominent family introduced him to distinguished political figures, writers, and painters, and who helped him gain the opportunity to paint such notables as Grover Cleveland and Millard Fillmore. He became friendly with the Buffalo painters Thomas Le Clear and William H. Beard, with whom he worked to establish the Buffalo Fine Arts Academy, which opened in 1862. Sellstedt was a self-educated man who also pursued interests in history, science, and anatomy. Before his death in 1911, he wrote a history of art in Buffalo, an autobiography, and a biography of his friend, the genre and portrait painter, William John Wilgus.

WALTER SHIRLAW (1838-1909)

In the early 1850s, Walter Shirlaw was apprenticed to a bank-note engraving company in New York, where his Scottish parents had settled in 1841, three years after his birth. Shirlaw turned to painting later in the decade and exhibited for the first time at the National and Pennsylvania Academies in 1861. Financial difficulties forced him to return to bank-note engraving, this time in Chicago, where he played an active role in the founding of the Chicago Art Institute. By 1870, he had saved enough money to make his long-awaited trip to Europe, and spent much of the next seven years in Munich, where he studied with Alexander Wagner, Arthur von Ramberg, and Wilhelm von Kaulbach. Upon his return to New York in 1877, he became one of the founders and the first president of the Society of American Artists, as well as the first paid instructor at the Art Students League. Later in his career, Shirlaw also painted murals for the World's Fair in Chicago and the Library of Congress, executed decorative schemes of painted panels and stained glass windows for private residences, and contributed charcoal illustrations to periodicals.

37.
Waterlilies
n.d., oil on canvas
20 x 30"

National Collection of Fine Arts
Washington, D. C.
Gift of William T. Evans

38.
The Basket of Apples
1818, oil on board
10 x 14"

Flint Institute of Arts
Flint, Michigan

ROBERT STREET (1796-1865)

Born in Germantown, Pennsylvania, in 1796, Robert Street worked in Philadelphia, where he painted a wide variety of subjects – portraits, landscapes, still lifes, and religious and historical pictures. He began exhibiting at The Pennsylvania Academy of the Fine Arts in 1815, showed his portraits in Washington, D. C., in 1824, and held an exhibition of two-hundred paintings, which included both his own work and examples by the "old masters," at the Artists' Fund Hall in Philadelphia in 1840. Street was a collector, owning canvases attributed to Peter Paul Rubens, Annibale Carracci, Anthony Van Dyck, and the Americans Jeremiah Paul and Gilbert Stuart. In 1835, William Dunlap reported Street's death – an error which the artist had the unique experience of drawing to the author's attention that same year. At least four of his six children became artists, but none of them lived up to the reputations of their illustrious namesakes, which included, among others, Claude and Rubens.

EDWARD R. THAXTER (1854-1881)

Born in Maine in 1854, Edward R. Thaxter lived in Boston until his departure for Florence in 1878. His brief career was relatively obscure, even in the 19th century since his best-known piece of sculpture, *Love's First Dream,* was included among the Italian works in the American Exhibition of Foreign Products, Arts, and Manufactures held in Boston in 1883! *Absent-mindedness* was reported to be the last piece upon which he worked before his death. He died in Naples at the age of twenty-seven, a victim of "brain fever."

39.
The Fury (Probably Meg Merrilies)
1881, marble
25 1/2 x 20"

Museum of Fine Arts
Boston, Massachusetts
William E. Nickerson Fund

JOHN ROLLIN TILTON   (1828-1888)

John Rollin Tilton departed for Italy in 1852 with the sculptor Paul Akers, and, after a brief residence in Florence, lived and worked in Rome until his death in 1888. Tuckerman tells us that "two subjects especially have been ... rendered by Tilton again and again, with a peculiar effectiveness all his own — Rome and Venice." A native of Loudon, New Hampshire, Tilton never attended an art school or studied with any painter, but was profoundly influenced by Titian, whose work he studied around 1860 in the Alpine village of Pieve di Cadore. At this time, Tilton began to make detailed sketches from nature and to paint carefully observed landscapes, which differed from his earlier work, where he had strived to capture such "evanescent splendors of Nature" as sunset on the Italian Campagna. Tilton achieved great popularity during his lifetime; he was patronized by wealthy American and English collectors. It was impossible to purchase one of his works, "each one being the fulfillment of a commission given long before."

40.
Landscape (Italian Ruins)
n.d., oil on canvas
20 x 15 7/16"

Collection Mr. Graham Williford
Fairfield, Texas

ALLEN TUCKER (1866-1939)

Born in Brooklyn, Allen Tucker attended the Columbia University School of Mines and practiced architecture with the firm of McIlvaine and Tucker between 1895 and 1904, after which time he devoted himself to painting. He studied painting at the Art Students League with John Twachtman, about whom he later wrote a book. His study with Twachtman and his annual summer trips to Europe in the 1890s caused him to adopt the impressionist style, which he used to depict his favorite scenes along the East Coast on the shores of Maine, Massachusetts, and New Jersey. He subsequently turned to expressionism and was called the American van Gogh. He associated with the progressive art movements of his period, such as The Eight, and helped produce the catalogue for the Armory Show in 1913. During World War I, he served in the American Red Cross in France and produced a volume of poems, *There and Here,* which deals with his war experiences. Tucker had a long and close association with the Art Students League, where he was an instructor and lecturer between 1920 and 1928. He is the author of several articles and books on art, notably *Design and Idea* (1930), where he urges young artists to "stay here and paint; to go abroad and learn — to come back here and create." Tucker the architect, artist, author, and teacher died in New York in 1939.

41.
Cornshucks and Windmill
1909, oil on canvas
30 x 36"

Newark Museum
Newark, New Jersey
Gift of the Allen Tucker Memorial, 1964

CARL VON MARR (1858-1936)

Born in Milwaukee, Wisconsin in 1858, Carl von Marr spent most of his artistic career in Germany. His American citizenship was so little known that when he returned to New York in 1909 for The Metropolitan Museum of Art's exhibition of modern German painting, many Americans were astonished to find that he spoke such fluent English — they had forgotten he was an American. Marr's neglect in his homeland is particularly surprising when one remembers that his painting *The Flagellants* was widely exhibited, causing a sensation, before it arrived in his home town in the 1890s.

Marr had studied with Henry Vianden in Milwaukee before leaving for Europe to study in Weimar, Berlin, and Munich, where he was a student of Max and Gabriel Lindenschmidt. In 1893, he became a professor at the Munich Academy, and in 1922, was elevated to the position of Director. Marr was particularly esteemed for his mural decorations, such as his *Allegory of Life* in the residence of Graf von Faber-Castell near Nuremberg. In 1936, he died in Munich, the city that had been his residence for the past fifty years.

42.
Christmas Eve
1884, oil on canvas
20 7/8 x 19 5/16"

Milwaukee Art Center
Milwaukee, Wisconsin

ROBERT WALTER WEIR (1803-1889)

Henry Tuckerman devotes an entire chapter of his *Book of the Artists* to Robert Walter Weir, explaining that his "isolated position... (at West Point has) tended for some time past to keep him from the public eye." Weir replaced Charles R. Leslie as instructor of drawing at West Point in 1834; in 1846, he became a professor, remaining at the Military Academy until his retirement in 1876. His students included talents as diverse as James Abbott McNeill Whistler, Seth Eastman, Ulysses S. Grant, and William T. Sherman.

Before assuming his teaching responsibilities, he was instructed by an English heraldic painter and studied art at the American Academy of Fine Arts as well as anatomy at New York University. He also visited the studio of John Wesley Jarves, where he met Henry Inman, later a close friend.

Beginning in 1824, he spent four years abroad, principally in Italy, where he shared quarters with the American sculptor, Horatio Greenough.

Although he painted landscapes and portraits as well as literary and genre pictures, his most famous painting is of an historical theme, the *Embarkation of the Pilgrims,* begun in 1836 and installed in the Rotunda of the Capitol in Washington, D. C., in 1843. Weir designed and built the Church of the Holy Innocents in Highland Falls, New York, with the funds which he received for this painting. He was an early practitioner of etching in America and made illustrations. By the time of his death in 1889, his two sons John Ferguson and Julian Alden Weir had already launched their successful artistic careers.

43.
The Microscope
1849, oil on canvas
30 x 40"

Yale University Art Gallery
New Haven, Connecticut
John Hill Morgan, B.A. 1893, and
Olive Louise Dann Funds, 1964.15

Bibliography

ABBREVIATED SOURCES

Bénézit   Bénézit, E. *Dictionnaire des Peintres, Sculpteurs, Dessinateurs et Gravures.* France, 1960.

Clement and Hutton   Clement [Waters], Clara Erskine, and Hutton, Laurence, eds. *Artists of the Nineteenth Century and Their Works.* 2 vols. Boston, 1879; reprinted New York, 1969 (Arno Press), 2 vols. in one, from 7th rev. ed., Boston and New York, 1894.

Groce and Wallace   Groce, George C., and Wallace, David H. *The New-York Historical Society's Dictionary of Artists in America,* 1564-1860. New Haven, 1957.

Tuckerman   Tuckerman, Henry T. *Book of the Artists.* New York, 1867; reprinted New York, 1966.

JOHN WHITE ALEXANDER

Alexander, Elizabeth. 'Whistler as We Knew Him," *American Magazine of Art,* 27 (September, 1934), sup. 16-17.

Blashfield, Edwin H. "John W. Alexander – Painter," *Art World,* 2 (September, 1917), 522-24.

Brinton, Christian. "The Art of John W. Alexander," *Munsey's Magazine,* 39 (September, 1908), 744-55.

Caffin, Charles H. "John W. Alexander," *Arts and Decoration,* 1 (February, 1911), 146-49, 178.

_____. "John W. Alexander: The Painter of Idealized Sentiment, through Portraits of Women in Poses," *World's Work,* 9 (January, 1905), 5682-98.

Catalogue of Paintings, John White Alexander Memorial Exhibition. Department of Fine Arts, Carnegie Institute, Pittsburgh, Pennsylvania, March, 1916.

Cortissoz, Royal. "The Decorations of Mr. Alexander," *Harper's Weekly,* 41 (January 23, 1897), 82-83.

Dayot, Armand. "John W. Alexander," *Harper's Magazine,* 99 (October, 1899), 694-704.

The Evolution of the Book as Illustrated by the Six Mural Paintings by John White Alexander in the Library of Congress. Baltimore, Maryland, 1965.

Farnsworth, P. T. "John W. Alexander, Artist: A Study in Determination," *Craftsman,* 10 (April, 1906), 46-53.

Harris, William Laurel. "John White Alexander, His Influence on American Art and Industry," *Good Furniture,* 5 (August, 1915), 63-73.

"How Whistler Posed for John W. Alexander," *World's Work,* (March, 1905), 5993-94.

John White Alexander memorial number. *American Magazine of Art,* 7 (July, 1916), including Edwin Howland Blashfield, "John W. Alexander, Recorder, Creator, Dreamer, and Friend," 345-48; Howard Russell Butler, "John W. Alexander, Organizer and Leader," 348-53; Charles Dana Gibson, "John W. Alexander, Illustrator and Man," 353; "John White Alexander: A Biographical Sketch," 355-60 (reprinted from the *Catalogue of Paintings, John White Alexander Memorial Exhibition,* Department of Fine Arts, Carnegie Institute, Pittsburgh, March, 1916); John W. Beatty, "John W. Alexander: A Reminiscence," 363-64; Homer Saint-Gaudens, "John W. Alexander in the Theater," 365-73.

"John White Alexander, N. A., The Man and His Work," *Scribner's Magazine,* 58 (September, 1915), 385-88. Tributes by Edward Robinson, Edwin H. Blashfield, Kenyon Cox, Howard Russell Butler, Harry W. Watrous.

"John White Alexander, Portrait-Painter, Decorator, Illustrator," *Critic,* 35 (July, 1899), 609-15.

Laurvik, John Nilsen. "John W. Alexander: An Analysis," *Metropolitan Magazine,* 31 (December, 1909), 369-76.

McSpadden, Joseph Walker, "John White Alexander: The Painter of the Flowing Line," in his *Famous Paintings of America.* New York, 1923, 355-76.

Monroe, Harriet. "John W. Alexander, His Paintings," *House Beautiful,* 15 (January, 1904), 66-74.

Morris, Harrison S. "The Portraits of John W. Alexander," *Scribner's Magazine,* 25 (March, 1899), 340-48.

Mourey, Gabriel. "An American Painter in Paris: John W. Alexander," *International Studio,* 11 (August, 1900), 71-77.

"The Pictures of John W. Alexander," *Harper's Weekly,* 46 (December 13, 1902), 1970-71.

Saint-Gaudens, Homer. "John W. Alexander," *Critic,* 46 (March, 1905), 238-39.

Testimonial to John W. Alexander, an address by John Agar, Fine Arts Federation of New York, New York 1916.

"A True Servant of Art," *Century Magazine,* 90 (October, 1915), 957-58.

Walton, William. "Alexander's Decorations," *Scribner's Magazine,* 45 (January, 1909), 45-57.

Weitenkampf, Frank. "John White Alexander, Artist and Citizen," *Bulletin of the New York Public Library,* 19 (July, 1915), 530-41.

Whitworth, Grace. "The Career of J. W. Alexander," *Fine Arts Journal,* 24 (January, 1911), 12-21.

ABRAHAM ARCHIBALD ANDERSON

Anderson, Abraham Archibald. *Experiences and Impressions; The*

Autobiography of Colonel A. A. Anderson. New York, 1933.

"Anderson's Paintings Shown at the Anderson Art Gallery at William and Mary," *Art Digest,* 5 (March 1, 1931), 6.

Bénézit, I, 156.

Clement and Hutton, I, 15-16.

"Col. A. A. Anderson, Artist, 93, Is Dead," *New York Times,* April 28, 1940.

"Colonel Anderson Dies; Artist and Indian Fighter," *New York Herald Tribune,* April 28, 1940.

Exhibition of Portraits by A. A. Anderson. Avery Galleries, New York, December 11-23, 1899.

"Mr. Anderson's Model Studio, A Modern and Beautiful Home of Art," *Town and Country,* 57 (May 3, 1902), 17-18.

FORTUNATO ARRIOLA

Groce and Wallace, 13-14.

Tropical Scenes by the 19th Century Painters of California, essay by Marjorie Arkelian. Oakland Museum, Oakland, California, October 5 - November 14, 1971.

JAMES H. BEARD

"American Painters. James H. Beard," *Art Journal,* n.s. 1 (1875), 366 68.

Catalogue of the collection of paintings and studies by the late James H. Beard...to be sold by auction...March 21st, 1895...by order of the executrix, at the Fifth Avenue Auction Rooms, 238 Fifth Avenue; and on that same day, 14 splendid examples from the studio of Mr. V. Tojetti. Also... March 20th and 22nd...by order of the People's Trust Company of Brooklyn, executor, and private individuals, 150 selected examples by celebrated American and European artists...Fifth Avenue Auction Rooms. New York, 1895.

Clement and Hutton, I, 43.

Groce and Wallace, 38.

"James H. Beard," *New York Times,* April 5, 1893.

Sheldon, George William. *American Painters.* New York, 1879, 113-17.

Smith, Winifred. "James Henry Beard," *Museum Echoes,* 27, no. 4 (April, 1954), 27-30.

Tuckerman, 436-37.

WILLIAM HOLBROOK BEARD

"American Painters: William H. Beard and Arthur Quartley," *Art Journal,* n.s. 4 (November, 1878), 321-24.

Baur, John I. H. "The Beard Movement," *Magazine of Art,* 43 (January, 1950), 16-17.

Beard, [William] H. *Action in Art.* New York, 1893.

_____ "An Artist's Reminiscences," *Harper's Magazine,* 62 (April, 1881), 699-701; 63 (September, 1881), 556-59.

_____ *Humor in Animals.* New York and London, 1885.

_____ *The Spade. Being an address in verse delivered at the annual dinner of the National Academy of Design,* New York, May 9, 1894.

Benjamin, Samuel G. W. "William H. Beard," in *Our American Artists.* Boston, 1886, 7-21.

_____ "William H. Beard, N. A.," in Wilfrid Meynell, ed., *Some Modern Artists.* London, 1883, 191-95.

Clement and Hutton, I, 43-44.

Groce and Wallace, 38.

Haverstock, M. S. "American Bestiary," *Art in America,* 58 (July-August, 1970), 37-71.

Sheldon, George William. *American Painters.* New York, 1879, 56-60.

Tuckerman, 498-501.

Viele, Chase. "Four Artists of Mid-Nineteenth Century Buffalo," *New York History,* 43 (January, 1962), 49-78.

ROBERT FREDERICK BLUM

Blum, Robert. "An Artist in Japan," *Scribner's Magazine,* 13 (April-June, 1893), 399-414, 624-36, 729-49.

Bridges, Robert. "Robert Frederick Blum," *The Lamp,* 26 (July, 1903), 473-77.

Caffin, Charles H. "Robert Frederick Blum," *International Studio,* 21 (December, 1903), clxxvii-cxcii.

_____, ed. "Mural painting by Robert F. Blum," *Artist,* 23 (October, 1898), xv-xvi.

Cortissoz, Royal. "Making of a Mural Decoration," *Century Magazine,* n.s. 37 59 (November, 1899), 58-63.

_____ *Personalities in Art.* London, 1925, 409-16.

"Decorative Painting by Blum, Mendelssohn Glee Club," *Scribner's Magazine,* 19 (January, 1896), 3-9.

Catalogue of a Memorial Loan Exhibition of the Works of Robert Frederick Blum, with an introduction by Martin Birnbaum. Berlin Photographic Gallery, New York, 1913.

"Etchings of Robert Frederick Blum," *Art in America,* 22 (December, 1933), 37-38.

McCabe, L. R. "Illustrated Epistolary Art of Robert Blum," *Arts and Decoration,* 4 (November, 1913), 20-23.

A Retrospective Exhibition of Robert F. Blum, introduction by Robert Boyle. Cincinnati Art Museum, April 1-May 7, 1966.

Weber, Bruce. "Robert Frederick Blum," projected Ph.D. thesis, research in progress, City University of New York.

ALFRED BOISSEAU

Bénézit, I, 738.

Groce and Wallace, 62.

The Louisiana Landscape 1800-1869. Anglo-American Art Museum, Louisiana State University, Baton Rouge, September 14-November 15, 1969.

Seebold, Herman. *Old Louisiana Plantation Homes and Family Trees.* New Orleans, 1941.

Wiesendanger, Martin, and Wiesendanger, Margaret. *Louisiana Painters and Paintings from the Collection of W. E. Groves.* New Orleans, 1971.

SAMUEL MARSDEN BROOKES

Butts, Porter. *Art in Wisconsin.* Madison, 1936.

Ely, Lydia. "Art and Artists in Milwaukee," in Howard Louis Conrad, *History of Milwaukee County.* Chicago, 1898.

Frankenstein, Alfred V. *After the Hunt.* 2nd ed. Berkeley and Los Angeles, 1969.

Gerdts, William H., and Burke, Russell. *American Still-Life Painting.* New York, 1971.

Marshall, Lucy Agar. "Samuel Marsden Brookes," *Wisconsin Magazine of History,* 52, no. 1 (Autumn, 1968), 51-59.

Pierce, Bessie L. *A History of Chicago.* New York and London, 1937-40.

Samuel Marsden Brookes, edited by Joseph Armstrong Baird, Jr. California Historical Society, San Francisco, November 10-December 29, 1962.

GEORGE LORING BROWN

"American Painters – George Loring Brown," *Art Journal,* n.s. 3 (1877), 370-72.

American Paintings: A Catalogue of the Collection of The Metropolitan Museum of Art, I, by Albert Ten Eyck Gardner and Stuart P. Feld. Greenwich, Conn., 1965, 275-77.

The Arcadian Landscape: Nineteenth Century American Painters in Italy, essay by Barbara Novak. University of Kansas Museum of Art, Lawrence,

Kansas, November 4-December 3, 1972.

Benjamin, Samuel G. W. "George Loring Brown," in his *Our American Artists.* Boston, c. 1886, 163-78.

Catalogue of the Large and Valuable Collection of Oil Paintings, Studies and Pencil Drawings, of Our Eminent American Artist, George L. Brown... Gallery of John Snedicor, New York, December 15-16, 186-(?).

Catalogue of the...Paintings, Studies and Pencil Drawings of...G. L. Brown...sold...1862 (?). Miner and Somerville, New York, 1862 (?).

Clement and Hutton, I, 102-03.

"George L. Brown," by T. R. K., *Zeitschrift für Bildende Kunst,* 6 (1871), 61-68.

"George Loring Brown," in Walter Montgomery, ed. *American Art and American Art Collections.* Vol. 2. Boston, 1889, 962-65.

George Loring Brown, Landscapes of Europe and America, 1834-1880, essays by Thomas W. Leavitt and William David Barry. The Robert Hull Fleming Museum, Burlington, Vermont, October 15-November 14, 1973.

"George Loring Brown's Account Book, 1851-1859," manuscript in the library of the Museum of Fine Arts, Boston.

Groce and Wallace, 85.

Harriet Peace Brown Papers. Archives of American Art, Smithsonian Institution, Washington, D. C.

Leavitt, Thomas W. "The Life, Work and Significance of George Loring Brown." Unpublished Ph.D. dissertation, Harvard University, 1957.

Marmor, Jarl Earl Marble(?). "Art in Boston," *The Aldine,* 8, no. 1 (January, 1876), 32.

Sheldon, George William. *American Painters.* New York, 1879, 111-13.

Tuckerman, 346-54.

WILLIAM MASON BROWN

Brooklyn Daily Eagle, September 6, 1898. [Obituary.]

Gerdts, William H. "Influence of Ruskin and Pre-Raphaelitism on American Still-Life Painting," *American Art Journal,* 1, no. 2 (Fall, 1969), 80-97.

_____, and Burke, Russell. *American Still-Life Painting.* New York, 1971.

Groce and Wallace, 90.

GEORGE DE FOREST BRUSH

Art Digest, 15 (May 1, 1941), 14; *Boston Globe,* April 25, 1941; *New York Times,* April 25, 1941. [Obituaries.]

Bowditch, Nancy Douglas. *George de Forest Brush.* Peterborough, New Hampshire, 1970.

Brush, George de Forest. "An Artist Among the Indians," *Century Magazine,* 30 (May, 1885), 54-7.

Caffin, Charles H. "George de Forest Brush," in *American Masters of Painting.* New York, 1902, 129-40.

Cortissoz, Royal. "George de Forest Brush," in *American Artists.* New York, 1923, 69-74.

Daingerfield, Elliott. "George de Forest Brush," *Art in America,* 18 (June, 1930), 214-18.

Ely, Catherine Beach. "George de Forest Brush," *Art in America,* 11

(June, 1923), 200-07.

_____ *The Modern Tendency in American Painting.* New York, 1925.

"George de Forest Brush," *Art World,* 2 (April, 1917), 8-9.

George de Forest Brush: Exhibition of Paintings and Drawings, November 1933-May 1934. American Academy of Arts and Letters, New York, 1933.

McCracken, Harold. *Portrait of the Old West.* New York, 1952.

Merrick, Lula. "Brush's Indian Pictures. American Painter Won Lasting Fame by the Spirituality of His Aboriginal Subjects," *International Studio,* 76 (December, 1922), 187-93.

Retrospective Exhibition of Paintings by George de Forest Brush. Grand Central Art Galleries, Inc., New York, January 7-18, 1930.

Saint-Gaudens, Homer. "Work of George de Forest Brush," *Critic,* 17 (August, 1905), 134-35.

"Six Modern American Portrait Painters," *Mentor,* 12 (October, 1924), 30-44.

Smith, Minna C. "George de Forest Brush," *International Studio,* 34 (April, 1908), xlvii-lvi.

DENNIS MILLER BUNKER

American Impressionist and Realist Paintings and Drawings from the Collection of Mr. and Mrs. Raymond Horowitz, introduction by John K. Howat and Diane H. Pilgrim. The Metropolitan Museum of Art, New York, April 19-June 3, 1973.

Cortissoz, Royal. "The Paintings of Dennis Miller Bunker," *New York Herald Tribune,* October 10, 1943.

Dennis Miller Bunker, Exhibition of Paintings and Drawings, preface by H. Ives Gammel. Museum of Fine Arts, Boston, 1943.

Gammel, H. Ives. *Dennis Miller Bunker.* New York, 1953.

GEORGE COMEGYS

"George Comegys," Artists' Files, Art Division, New York Public Library,

New York.

Groce and Wallace, 142.

"A Philadelphia Genre Painter [Harry Shaw Newman Gallery]," *Panorama,* 1 (June-July, 1946), 106-07.

Tuckerman, 494.

Williams, Hermann Warner. *Mirror to the American Past.* Greenwich, Connecticut, 1973.

S. S. DAVID

Childe, Cromwell. "A Painter of Pretty Women." *The Quarterly Illustrator,* 1 (October, November, and December, 1893), 279-82.

Clements and Hutton, I, 242-44.

Frankenstein, Alfred V. *After the Hunt,* 2d ed. Berkeley and Los Angeles, 1969.

Gerdts, William H., and Burke, Russell. *American Still-Life Painting.* New York, 1971.

Groce and Wallace, 166.

Peat, Wilbur D. *Pioneer Paintings of Indiana.* Indianapolis, 1954.

SARAH PAXTON BALL DODSON

"Acquisitions," *Bulletin of the Boston Museum of Fine Arts,* 22 (February, 1924), 7.

Bye, Arthur Edwin. "Three Paintings by Sarah Ball Dodson," *Pennsylvania Museum Bulletin,* 21, no. 102 (April, 1926), 135-36.

Catalogue of the Exhibition of Paintings by Sarah Ball Dodson. American Art Galleries, New York, December 16-29, 1911.

Catalogue of Paintings by Sarah B. Dodson, essay by J. E. D. T. [John E. D. Trask]. Pennsylvania Academy of the Fine Arts, Philadelphia, April 16-May 14, 1911.

[Sturgis, Russell]. "The Work of Miss Sarah Dodson," *Scribner's Magazine,* 43 (April, 1908), 509-12.

Trask, John E. D. "Sarah Ball Dodson: An Appreciation," *International Studio,* 45 (December, 1911), xxxvii-xli.

HENRY F. FARNY

"Among the Artists," *American Art News,* V. 5., no. 24 (March 30, 1907), n.p.

Clark, Edna M. *Ohio Art and Artists.* Richmond, 1932.

Cushing, Drank, with illustrations by Henry Farny. "My Adventures in Zuni," *Century Magazine,* n.s. 3 (December, 1882), 191-207; (February,

1883), 500-11; n.s. 4 (May, 1883), 28-47.

Flynn, Edward F. (?) "The Paintings of H. F. Farny — Something about the Career of the Eminent Cincinnati Artist," *Cincinnati Commercial Gazette,* March 14, 1893.

Goss, Rev. C. F. *Cincinnati, Queen City.* Chicago and Cincinnati, 1912.

Henry Farny and the American Indian. Cincinnati Art Museum, March 2-April 4, 1943.

Loan Exhibition of Paintings by Henry F. Farny, essay by L. H. Meakin.

Cincinnati Museum, April 24-May 16, 1915.

McCracken, Harold. *Portrait of the Old West.* New York, 1952.

McLaughlin, George. "Cincinnati Artists of the Munich School," *American Art Review,* 2 (November, 1881), 1-4; 45-50; also printed in Walter Montgomery, ed., *American Art and American Art Collections.* Vol. 1. Boston, 1889, 145-60.

Smalley, Eugene V., with illustrations by Henry Farny. "The Upper Missouri and the Great Falls," *Century Magazine,* n.s. 13 (January, 1888), 408-18.

Taft, Robert. "The Pictorial Record of the Old West; X. Artists of Indian Life: Henry F. Farny," *The Kansas Historical Quarterly,* 18, no. 1 (February, 1950), 1-19; reprinted as: Robert Taft. *Artists of Indian Life: Henry F. Farny.* Pictorial Record of the Old West, 10. Topeka, Kansas, 1950.

MANUEL JOACHIM DE FRANCA

Groce and Wallace, 237-38.

Sartain, John. *The Reminiscences of a Very Old Man, 1808-1897.* New York, 1899.

WALTER GAY

Allen, J. L. "Memorial Exhibition of Paintings by Walter Gay," *Metropolitan Museum Bulletin,* 33 (April, 1938), 100-02.

Catalogue of an Exhibition of Oil Paintings and Water Colors by Walter Gay. The Buffalo Fine Arts Academy, Albright Art Gallery, Buffalo, New York, May 10-September 14, 1913.

Child, Theodore. "Gallery and Studio — Walter Gay," *Art Amateur,* 14 (December, 1885), 57-58.

Clement and Hutton, I, 287.

Fitz-Gibbon, Costen. "Paintings of French Interiors by Walter Gay," *Arts and Decoration Quarterly,* 1 (Summer, 1929), 16-17, 100.

Gallatin, Albert Eugene. *Certain Contemporaries: A Set of Notes in Art Criticism.* New York, 1916.

_____. "Mr. Walter Gay's Interiors," *Art and Progress,* 4 (July, 1913), 1023-27.

_____, ed. *Walter Gay – Paintings of French Interiors.* New York, 1920.

Gay, Walter. *Memoirs of Walter Gay.* New York, 1930.

Gillet, Louis. "Peintres d'Amerique – Walter Gay," *Revue de L'Art Ancien et Moderne,* Tome 39 (January, 1921), 32-44.

Huyghe, Rene. "La Donation Walter Gay au Musée du Louvre," *Bulletin des Musées de France,* 10 (January-February, 1938), 6-8.

Lane, James W. "Walter Gay," *Art in America,* 26 (January, 1938), 24-28.

Memorial Exhibition of Paintings by Walter Gay. The Metropolitan Museum of Art, New York, April 9-May 30, 1938.

"Paintings of Old French Interiors," *Arts and Decoration,* 34 (March, 1931), 40-41.

Walter Gay. Graham Gallery, New York, January 5-February 15, 1974.

SAMUEL LANCASTER GERRY

Bolton, Theodore. "Early American Portrait Painters in Oil," unpublished manuscript, at the New-York Historical Society.

Clement and Hutton, I, 292.

Gerry, Samuel Lancaster. "Artists in Florence and Rome in 1849-50," unpublished manuscript in the Frick Art Reference Library, New York.

_____. "Old Masters of Boston," *New England Magazine,* n.s. 3 (February, 1891), 682-95.

_____. "On Framing and Hanging Pictures," *New England Magazine,* n.s. 4 (July, 1891), 647-48.

_____. "Reminiscences of the Boston Art Club," manuscript in the Boston Athenaeum.

Groce and Wallace, 255.

Tuckerman, 566.

EDWARD WILBUR DEAN HAMILTON

American Paintings, catalogue by Barbara Neville Parker and Arianwen Howard. Museum of Fine Arts, Boston, 1969.

Catalogue of the Fifteenth Exhibition, 1893. Society of American Artists, American Fine Arts Society, New York, April 17-May 13, 1893.

Impressionism in America. University of New Mexico Art Gallery, Albuquerque, New Mexico, February 9-March 14, 1965.

JAMES HAMILTON

Baur, John I. H. "A Romantic Impressionist: James Hamilton," *Brooklyn Museum Bulletin,* 12 (Spring, 1951), 1-9.

Clement and Hutton, I, 327.

Gordon, John. "James Hamilton, A Forgotten Painter," *Art in America,* 44 (Fall, 1956), 15-17, 56.

_____ "Two Paintings by James Hamilton, 1819-1878: *Last Days of Pompeii, Foundering,*" *Brooklyn Museum Bulletin,* 17, no. 4 (Summer, 1956), 1.

Groce and Wallace, 287.

James Hamilton, 1819-1878, essay by Arlene Jacobitz. Brooklyn Museum, Brooklyn, New York, March 28-May 22, 1966.

Mastai, M. L. D. "James Hamilton, American Marine Painter," *Connoisseur,* 163 (September, 1966), 66-67.

Tuckerman, 565-66.

HARRIET HOSMER

"The Beatrice Cenci," *The Crayon,* 4, part 12 (December, 1857), 379.

Bidwell, W. H. "Harriet G. Hosmer," *Eclectic Magazine,* 77 (August, 1871), 245-46.

Bradford, Ruth A. "The Life and Works of Harriet Hosmer," *New England Magazine,* n.s, 15, no. 2 (October, 1911), 265-69.

Carr, Cornelia, ed. *Harriet Hosmer, Letters and Memories.* New York, 1912.

Child, L. Maria. "Miss Harriet Hosmer," *Littell's Living Age,* 56, no. 720 (March 13, 1858), 697-98.

Clement and Hutton, I, 366-67.

Craven, Wayne. *Sculpture in America.* New York, 1968.

Groce and Wallace, 328.

"Harriet Hosmer," *Cosmopolitan Art Journal,* 3, no. 5 (December, 1859), 214-17.

Hosmer, Harriet. "The Process of Sculpture," *Atlantic Monthly,* 14, no. 86 (December, 1864), 734-37.

"Miss Hosmer's Statue of Zenobia," *The New Path,* 2, no. 4 (April, 1865), 49-53.

"Puck," *The Art Journal,* n.s. 14 (1875), 312.

Taft, Lorado. *The History of American Sculpture.* New York, 1925.

Thurston, Reverend R. B. "Harriet Hosmer," in J. Porton, H. Greeley, T. W. Higginson, et al. *Eminent Women of the Age.* Hartford, 1869, 566-98.

Tuckerman, 601-02.

Van Rensselaer, Susan. "Harriet Hosmer," *Antiques,* 84, no. 4 (October, 1963), 424-28.

The White Marmorean Flock: Nineteenth Century American Women Neoclassical Sculptors, essay by William H. Gerdts. Vassar College Art Gallery, Poughkeepsie, New York, April 4-30, 1972.

DAVID JOHNSON

Catalogue of Paintings in Oil by David Johnson, N. A. To be sold at auction... February 13th-14th...at Fifth Avenue Art Galleries... Ortgies & Co., New York, 1890.

Clement and Hutton, II, 11.

"David Johnson," *Buffalo Academy Notes,* 3, no. 10 (March, 1908), 179.

"David Johnson Dead," *American Art News,* 6, no. 16 (February 1, 1908), 1.

Groce and Wallace, 352.

Miller, Jo. "Drawings of the Hudson River School: The Second Generation, Part 2," *Connoisseur,* 175 (September, 1970), 47-55.

GEORGE COCHRAN LAMBDIN

Bolton, Theodore. *Early American Portrait Draughtsmen in Crayons.* New York, 1923; reprinted by Kennedy Graphics, Inc., Da Capo Press, New York, 1970.

Clement and Hutton, II, 32.

Gerdts, William H., and Burke, Russell. *American Still-Life Painting.* New York, 1971.

Groce and Wallace, 381.

Tuckerman, 450-51.

Williams, Hermann Warner. *Mirror to the American Past.* Greenwich, Connecticut, 1973.

MARTIN J. LAWLER

Frankenstein, Alfred. *After the Hunt.* 2d ed. Berkeley and Los Angeles, 1969, 159.

Gerdts, William H., and Burke, Russell. *American Still-Life Painting.* New York, 1971.

ALEXANDER LAWRIE

"Alexander Lawrie," Artists' Files, Art and Architecture Division, New York Public Library, New York.

Clement and Hutton, II, 43-4.

Gibbens, Victor E. "Alexander Lawrie, Painter," *Indiana Magazine of History*, 40 (March, 1944), 33-40.

Groce and Wallace, 388.

Tuckerman, 566.

JERVIS MCENTEE

Aldrich, Thomas. "Among the Studios," *Our Young Folks*, Vol. 2. Boston, 1866, 622-25.

"American Painters – Jervis McEntee, N.A.," *Art Journal*, n.s. 2 (1876), 178-79.

Catalogue of a Choice Collection of Original Pictures by Jervis McEntee, S. Colman, and A. B. Shattuck...to be sold at auction...April 12, 1864... Allen B. Miner and Brother, New York, 1864.

Catalogue of Paintings of the Late Jervis McEntee, N. A. ... Sold... March 29th and 30th... Ortgies & Co., New York, 1892.

Clement and Hutton, II, 104-45.

Gerdts, William H. "Reattributions: Church, Healy, McEntee's the Arch of Titus." *Museum* (Newark), n.s. 10, no. 1 (Winter, 1958), 18-20.

Groce and Wallace, 412-13.

Jervis McEntee. American Landscape Painter. Born at Rondout, New York, 1828; Member National Academy of Design, 1861; died January 27, 1891, a memorial address by John F. Weir. New York, 1891.

"The Jervis McEntee Diary," *Journal of the Archives of American Art*, 8, nos. 3 & 4 (July-October, 1968), 1-29.

Jervis McEntee Papers, Archives of American Art, Smithsonian Institution, Washington, D.C.

Sheldon, George William. *American Painters.* New York, 1879, 51-56.

Tuckerman, 543-46.

FREDERICK MACMONNIES

American Architect and Architecture, 150 (April, 1937), 143; *Art Digest*, 11 (April 1, 1937), 22. [Obituary.]

American Sculptors. Scrapbook of Reproductions, Frederick MacMonnies. New York Public Library, 1931.

"Art and the Public: 'Civic Virtue,' Mr. MacMonnies' Statue for City Hall Fountain, New York," *Architecture*, 45 (April, 1922), 117, frontispiece.
Brinton, Christian. "Frederick MacMonnies," *Munsey's Magazine*, 34 (February, 1906), 415-22.
Caffin, Charles H. "Mr. Frederick MacMonnies's Group for Prospect Park, Brooklyn," *Harper's Weekly*, 41 (July 31, 1897), 753.

Cortissoz, Royal. "An American Sculptor: Frederick MacMonnies," *Studio,* 6 (October, 1895), 17-26.

_____ "Some Imaginative Types in American Art," *Harper's Monthly,* 91 (July, 1895), 164-79.

Craven, Wayne. *Sculpture in America.* New York, 1968.

Dreiser, Theodore. "Art of MacMonnies and [William] Morgan," *Metropolitan,* 7 (February, 1898), 143-51.

"Frederick MacMonnies," Artists' Files, Art and Architecture Division, New York Public Library, New York.

Frederick William MacMonnies Papers, Archives of American Art, Smithsonian Institution, Washington, D. C.

"Frederick MacMonnies," *Critic,* 31, n.s. 28 (July 3, 1897), 1-3.

Greer, H. H. "Frederick MacMonnies, Sculptor," *Brush and Pencil,* 10 (April, 1902), 1-15.

King, Pauline. "A Painting by Frederick MacMonnies," *Century Magazine,* 66 (August, 1903), 528, 637-38.

Low, Will H. "Frederick MacMonnies," *Scribner's Magazine,* 18 (November, 1895), 617-28.

MacMonnies, Frederick. "Glory of France in Sculpture," *World's Work,* 34 (October, 1917), 601.

"The MacMonnies Pioneer Monument for Denver: An Embodiment of the Western Spirit," *Century Magazine,* 80 (October, 1910), 875-80.

Meltzer, Charles Mercer. "Frederick MacMonnies, Sculptor," *Cosmopolitan,* 53 (July, 1912), 207-11.

"New Works by MacMonnies," *Critic,* 26, n.s. 23 (February 16, 1895), 129.

Payne, Frank O. "Famous Statues by American Sculptors: Shakespeare as Pictured by Ward, Partridge and MacMonnies," *International Studio,* 58 (April, 1916), xxxvii-xliv.

Pettit, Edith. "Frederick MacMonnies, Portrait Painter," *International Studio,* 29 (October, 1906), 319-24.

Quélin, René de. "Early Days with MacMonnies in St. Gaudens' Studio. A Personal Reminiscence," *Arts and Decoration,* 16 (April, 1922), 424-25; 479.

Strother, French. "Frederick MacMonnies, Sculptor," *World's Work,* 2 (December, 1905), 6965-81.

LOUIS REMY MIGNOT

Catalogue of a Choice Collection of Paintings and Studies from Nature, Painted by Louis R. Mignot...to be Sold at Auction...on the Evening of Monday, June 2nd, 1862, at the Gallery of J. Snedicor. New York, 1892.

Clement and Hutton, II, 114-15.

*A Description of the Home of Washington after the War: Painted by T. P.
Rossiter and L. R. Mignot. With Historical Sketches of the Personages
Introduced...by R. [Thomas Rossiter?].* New York, 1859.

Groce and Wallace, 442.

Tuckerman, 563-64.

LOUIS MOELLER

Art Digest, 5 (November 15, 1930), 5; *Art News,* 29 (November 22,
1930), 14. [Obituary.]

Ruckstuhl, F. Wellington. "A Sculptor's Opinion of a Painter," *Quarterly
Illustrator,* 2 (October, November, and December, 1894), 345-52.

Sheldon, George William. *Recent Ideals of American Art.* New York,
1888.

Williams, Hermann Warner. *Mirror to the American Past.* Greenwich,
Connecticut, 1973.

SAMUEL MURRAY

Art Digest, 16 (January 1, 1942), 12; *New York Times,* November 4,
1941. [Obituary.]

Breckenridge, James D. "Thomas Eakins' Portrait of Mrs. Samuel
Murray," *Baltimore Museum News,* 19 (December, 1955), 6-15.

McHenry, Margaret. *Thomas Eakins Who Painted.* Oreland (?),
Pennsylvania, 1946.

Moffett, Cleveland. "Grant and Lincoln in Bronze," *McClure's Magazine,*
5 (October, 1895), 419-32.

Paintings by Thomas Eakins — Sculpture by Samuel Murray. The Fifty-
sixth Street Galleries, New York, January 17, 1931.

"Samuel Murray's Portrait of Eakins," *Detroit Institute Bulletin,* 40, no.
3-4 (1960-61), 51.

The Sculpture of Thomas Eakins, essay by Moussa Domit. Corcoran
Gallery of Art, Washington, D. C., May 3-June 10, 1969.

"Tales about Eakins Told to Henry McBride by Mr. Samuel Murray,
Sculptor and Eakins' Friend," Henry McBride Papers, Archives of
American Art, Smithsonian Institution, Washington, D. C.

THOMAS BUCHANAN READ

Brinton, Christian, et al. *Yesterday in Chester County Art.* Sponsored by
the Chester County Art Association and the School Board of West
Chester; Art Center, West Chester, Pennsylvania, 1936.

Clement and Hutton, II, 201-02.

Grigaut, Paul L. "An American Painter's Dream," *Detroit Institute Bulletin,* 38, no. 4 (1958-59), 89-91.

Groce and Wallace, 527.

Keller, I. C. "Thomas Buchanan Read," *Pennsylvania History,* 6 (July, 1939), 133-46.

Nathans, David. "Thomas Buchanan Read, Poet and Painter, 1822-1872; Selected Letters and Catalogue of Paintings." Master's essay in preparation, University of Delaware, Newark, Delaware, 1974.

Peasants, Henry, Jr. *Four Great Artists of Chester County.* West Chester, Pennsylvania, 1936.

Tait, John R. "Reminiscences of a Poet-Painter," *Lippincott's Magazine,* 19 (March, 1877), 207-321.

Townsend, Henry C. *A Memoir of T. Buchanan Read.* Philadelphia, 1889.

Tuckerman, 460-61.

ROBERT REID

American Impressionist Painting, essay by Moussa M. Domit. National Gallery of Art, Washington, D. C., 1973.

Art Digest, 4 (December 15, 1929), 13; *Art News,* 28 (December 7, 1929), 14; *New York Sun* (December 3, 1929); *New York Times* (December 3, 1929); *New York Tribune* (December 3, 1929). [Obituary.]

The Art Student. Vol. 1, Boston, 1882-84. Published irregularly by students in the School of Drawing and Painting, Museum of Fine Arts, Boston; Robert Reid, ed., June-December, 1882.

Brinton, Christian. "Robert Reid, Decorative Impressionist," *Arts and Decoration,* 2 (November, 1911), 13-15, 34.

Coffin, W. A. "Robert Reid's Decorations in the Congressional Library, Washington, D. C.," *Harper's Weekly,* 40 (October 17, 1896), 1028-29.

Cortissoz, Royal. *In Summertime: Paintings by Robert Reid.* New York, 1900.

_____ "The Work of Robert Reid," *Appleton's Booklover's Magazine,* 6 (December, 1905), 738-46.

Exhibition of Pictures by Robert Reid. Montross Gallery, New York, January 3-18, 1918.

Goodrich, Henry W. "Robert Reid and His Work," *International Studio,* 36 (February, 1909), cxiii-cxxii.

Hart, Charles Henry. "Robert Reid's Mural Decoration in the New State House at Boston," *Era,* n.s. 9 (April, 1902), 444-47.

Hoeber, Arthur. "Open Letters – Robert Reid," *Century Magazine,* 77 (March, 1909), 799.

Paintings by Robert Reid, introduction by Frank Crowninshield. Grand

Central Art Galleries, New York, April 1-14, 1927.

Pattison, James William. "Robert Reid, Painter," *House Beautiful,* 20 (July, 1906), 18-20.

Sargent, I. "Mural Paintings by Robert Reid in the Massachusetts State House," *Craftsman,* 7 (March, 1905), 699-712.

Stoner, Stanley. *Some Recollections of Robert Reid.* Colorado Springs, Colorado, 1934.

Stuart, Evelyn Marie. "Finished Impressions of a Portrait Painter," *Fine Arts Journal,* 36 (January, 1918), 33-40.

THOMAS P. ROSSITER

Bevan, Edith Rossiter. *Thomas Pritchard Rossiter 1818-1871.* Ruxton, Maryland, 1957.

_____. "Thomas Pritchard Rossiter." Manuscript in the Frick Art Reference Library, New York.

Brumbaugh, T. B. "Venice Letter from Thomas P. Rossiter," *American Art Journal,* 5 (May, 1973), 74-78.

Catalogue of Rossiter's Collection of Pictures and Sketches, to be Sold at Auction, by Thomas J. Miller...December 20th, 1859...at the National Academy of Design. New York, 1859.

Clement, Clara Erskine. "Early Religious Painting in America," *New England Magazine,* 9 (December, 1894), 387-402.

Clement and Hutton, II, 224-25.

A Description of Five Serial Pictures, Illustrating Milton's Paradise Lost, Painted by Thomas Rossiter. New York, 1865.

A Description of Three Scriptural Pictures, Jeremiah...Noah...Miriam... Painted by T. P. Rossiter. New York, 1860.

A Description of the Picture of the Home of Washington after the War. Painted by T. P. Rossiter and L. R. Mignot. New York, 1859.

French, Henry Willard. *Art and Artists in Connecticut.* New York, 1879.

Groce and Wallace, 548.

Rossiter's Great Scriptural Painting of the Return of the Dove, or the Triumph of Faith. The Pennsylvania Academy of the Fine Arts, Philadelphia, n.d.

Thomas Pritchard Rossiter: Paintings, Studies, Sketches. Messrs. Leavitt, New York, April 24, 1868.

Tuckerman, 435-36.

CHRISTIAN SCHUSSELE

"Art: Mr. Irving and His Literary Friends," *The Round Table,* 1, no. 2 (December 26, 1862), 27.

"Christian Schussele," Artists' Files, Art and Architecture Division, New York Public Library, New York.

Dewey, George W. "C. Schussele," *Sartain's Magazine,* 10 (June, 1852), 462-63.

Groce and Wallace, 564-65.

Johnston, Rev. George H. *A Sermon Memorial to Christian Schussele, for Eleven Years Professor of Drawing and Painting in the Pennsylvania Academy of the Fine Arts, Philadelphia.* Philadelphia, 1879.

"Men of Progress," *Scientific American,* 75 (July 25, 1896), 60-61.

Sartain, John. *Reminiscences of a Very Old Man.* New York, 1899.

Williams, Hermann Warner. *Mirror to the American Past.* Greenwich, Connecticut, 1973.

LARS SELLSTEDT

Clement and Hutton, II, 249.

Groce and Wallace, 568-69.

"Lars Gustaf Sellstedt," *Buffalo Academy Notes,* 4, no. 3 (July, 1911), 68-69.

Paintings by Lars Gustaf Sellstedt, essay by Walter McCausland. Buffalo Fine Arts Academy, Albright Art Gallery, Buffalo, May 23-July 3, 1962.

Sellstedt, Lars Gustaf. *Art in Buffalo.* Buffalo, 1910.

_____ *From Forecastle to Academy, Sailor and Artist: Autobiography.* Buffalo, 1904.

_____ *Life and Works of William John Wilgus, Artist, 1819-1853* (elected to The National Academy of Design, 1839). Buffalo, 1912.

Sprague, Henry W. "Lars Gustaf Sellstedt," *Publications of the Buffalo Historical Society,* 17 (Buffalo, 1913), 37-74.

"A Veteran Artist, Lars Sellstedt, N. A.," *Buffalo Academy Notes,* 3, no. 4 (September, 1907), 54-57.

Viele, Charles. "Four Artists in Mid-Nineteenth Century Buffalo," *New York History,* 43, no. 1 (January, 1962), 49-78.

WALTER SHIRLAW

"American Painters: Walter Shirlaw and F. Hopkinson Smith," *Art Journal,* (New York), n.s. 4 (1878), 360-63.

American Painters of the Munich School. Scrapbook of Reproductions. New York Public Library, 1934.

Bartlett, Truman Howe. "Walter Shirlaw," in Walter Montgomery, ed. *American Art and American Art Collections,* 1 (Boston, 1889), 53-63, 66-77; reprinted in *American Art Review,* 2, pt. 2 (1881), 97-102, 145-49.

Benjamin, Samuel G. W. *Our American Artists.* Boston, 1886, 88-103.

Catalogue of a Memorial Exhibition of Paintings and Drawings by Walter Shirlaw. Carnegie Institute, Pittsburgh, February 1-23, 1911.

Clement and Hutton, II, 251-52.

Dreier, Dorothea. "Walter Shirlaw," *Art in America,* 7 (Autumn, 1919), 206-16.

Groce and Wallace, 577.

"Memorial Exhibition of the Works of the Late Walter Shirlaw, N. A.," *Buffalo Academy Notes,* 6, no. 1 (January, 1911), 30-32.

Searle, A. T. "Walter Shirlaw Memorial Exhibition," *International Studio,* 43 (May, 1911), sup. 70-71.

Sheldon, George William. *American Painters.* New York, 1879, 96-97.

Shirlaw, Walter. "Artists' Adventures: The Rush to Death," *Century Magazine,* 47, n.s. 25 (November, 1893), 41-45.

Shirlaw, Mrs. Walter. "Biographical Sketch of Walter Shirlaw," *Aesthetics* (Muskegon, Michigan), 1, no. 4 (July, 1913), 64-67.

"Walter Shirlaw," *Bulletin of the Brooklyn Institute of Arts and Sciences,* 5, no. 6 (October 15, 1910), 127-29.

ROBERT STREET

Anderson, Edward P. "Intellectual Life of Pittsburgh, 1786-1836; VII: Painting," *Western Pennsylvania Historical Magazine,* 14 (October, 1931), 289-93.

Fielding, Mantle. "Robert Street, Artist," *Pennsylvania Magazine of History and Biography,* 45 (1921), 255-56.

Gerdts, William H., and Burke, Russell. *American Still-Life Painting.* New York, 1971.

Groce and Wallace, 610.

Semon, Kurt M. "Who Was Robert Street?" *American Collector,* 14 (June, 1945), 6-7, 19.

Sherman, Frederic Fairchild. "Portraits and Miniatures by Copley, Dunlap, Eicholtz and Robert Street," *Art in America,* 16 (April, 1928), 122-29.

Street, Mary E. A. *The Street Genealogy.* Exeter, New Hampshire, 1895.

Tuckerman, 494.

EDWARD R. THAXTER

American Exhibition of Foreign Products, Arts and Manufactures, Catalogue, Art Department. Boston, 1883.

Bénézit, 8, 267.

"The First Dream of Love," *Art Review,* 1 (December, 1886), illustration following p. 24.

"Necrology – Edward R. Thaxter," *American Art Review,* 2, part 2 (1881), 175.

Thieme-Becker, 32, 585.

JOHN ROLLIN TILTON

Akers, Paul. "Our Artists in Italy: Landscape Art," *Atlantic Monthly,* 9 (February, 1862), 162-70.

Clement and Hutton, II, 297-98.

Groce and Wallace, 631.

"J. Rollin Tilton," in Walter Montgomery, ed. *American Art and American Art Collections.* Vol. 2, Boston, 1889, 908-12.

James, Henry. *William Wetmore Story and His Friends.* 2 vols. Boston, 1903.

Neal, John. "Our Painters, II," *Atlantic Monthly,* 23 (March, 1869), 337-46.

Tuckerman, 558-59.

ALLEN TUCKER

Allen Tucker, with a note by Mildred Palmer. The Arts Portfolio Series, New York, 1930.

Allen Tucker, 1866-1966. Milch Galleries, New York, March 29-April 16, 1966.

Allen Tucker Memorial Exhibition, essay by Forbes Watson. Whitney Museum of American Art, New York, December 6, 1939-January 3, 1940.

Barker, Virgil. "The Paintings of Allen Tucker," *The Arts,* 13 (February, 1928), 75-88.

Exhibition of Paintings, Sketches and Drawings by Kenneth Frazier, Birge Harrison, William H. Hyde, Allen Tucker. Century Club, New York, February 17-March 1, 1909.

Lane, James W. "Vincent in America: Allen Tucker," *Art News,* 38 (December 16, 1939), 13, 17-18.

Tucker, Allen. "The Creative Attitude," *The Arts,* 16 (January, 1930), 293-300.

_____. *Design and the Idea.* New York, 1930.

_____ "The Essentials of Design," *The Arts,* 16 (February, 1930), 385-89, 438.

_____ *John H. Twachtman.* American Artists Series, Whitney Museum of American Art, New York, 1931.

Watson, Forbes. *Allen Tucker.* American Artists Series, Whitney Museum of American Art, New York, 1932.

150

_____ "Allen Tucker," *Magazine of Art,* 32 (December, 1939), 698-703.

_____ "Allen Tucker: A Painter with a Fresh Vision," *International Studio,* 52 (March, 1914), xix-xxi.

CARL VON MARR

American Painters of the Munich School. Scrapbook of Reproductions. New York Public Library, 1934.

"Exhibition of Drawings and Paintings by Professor Carl von Marr," *Milwaukee Art Institute Bulletin,* 2 (June-July, 1929), 2-4.

Fraser, W. Lewis. "American Artist Series," *Century Magazine,* 44, n.s. 22, (May, 1892), 100-03.

J., W. G. "Carl von Marr, der neue Präsident der münchner Künsterenossenschaft," *Die Kunst für Alle,* 30 (February, 1915), 188.

Marr, Carl [von]. "Great German Artist: Adolph Menzel," *Century Magazine,* 43, n.s. 21 (November, 1891), 17-27.

New York Times, July 11, 1936. [Obituary.]

Ostini, Fritz v. "Carl Marr," *Velhagen & Klasings Monatshefte,* 23 (September, 1908), 33-46.

Smith, Holmes. "Some New Decorative Paintings by Prof. Carl Marr," *International Studio,* 42 (November, 1910), 35-39.

Spier, Anna. "Carl Marr," *Die Kunst unserer Zeit,* 12, no. 1 (1901), 1-39.

Wolf, Georg Jacob. "Carl von Marr," *Die Kunst für Alle,* 26 (1910), 97-109.

ROBERT WEIR

Ahrens, Kent. "Religious Paintings of Robert Walter Weir," *Antiques,* 103 (April, 1973), 744-49.

_____ "Robert Walter Weir." Unpublished Ph.D. dissertation, University of Delaware, Newark, Delaware, 1972.

American Paintings: A Catalogue of the Collection of The Metropolitan Museum of Art, 1, by Albert Ten Eyck Gardner and Stuart P. Feld. Greenwich, Connecticut, 1965, 235-36.

Catalogue of Oil Paintings and Water Colors by Robert W. Weir, also His Collection of Engravings, Etchings, Illustrated Books... Fifth Avenue Art Galleries, New York, February 19-21, 1891.

Dunlap, William. *History of the Rise and Progress of the Arts of Design in the United States,* New York, 1834; reprinted with an introduction by William H. Campbell, New York, 1965.

Groce and Wallace, 669.

"Our Artists, no. VI: Weir," *Godey's Lady's Book,* 34 (February, 1847), 68-72.

The Picture of the Embarcation of the Pilgrims from Delft-Haven in Holland. New York, 1843.

"Robert W. Weir, N. A.," *Harper's Weekly,* 33, no. 1692 (May 25, 1889), 419-20.

Sheldon, George William. *American Painters.* New York, 1879, 160-64.

Tuckerman, 203-15.

Vail, R. W. G. "Encore for Santa," *New-York Historical Society Quarterly,* 37 (October, 1953), 26-30.

_____ "Santa Claus Visits the Hudson," *New-York Historical Society Quarterly,* 35 (October, 1951), 336-43.

Webber, Richard. "Birthplace of Robert Weir, Artist," *New-York Historical Society Quarterly,* 14 (October, 1940), 94.

Weir, Irene. *Robert W. Weir, Artist.* New York, 1947.